BOULEVARD OF BROKEN DREAMS

KAUFFMAN FOUNDATION SERIES ON
Innovation and Entrepreneurship

Boulevard of Broken Dreams: Why Public Efforts to Boost Entrepreneurship and Venture Capital Have Failed —and What to Do About It, by Josh Lerner

The Invention of Enterprise: Entrepreneurship from Ancient Mesopotamia to Modern Times, edited by David S. Landes, Joel Mokyr, and William J. Baumol

BOULEVARD OF BROKEN DREAMS

Why Public Efforts to

Boost Entrepreneurship

and Venture Capital Have Failed

—and What to Do About It

JOSH LERNER

PRINCETON UNIVERSITY PRESS

PRINCETON, NEW JERSEY

Published by Princeton University Press,
41 William Street, Princeton,
New Jersey 08540
In the United Kingdom: Princeton University Press,
6 Oxford Street, Woodstock, Oxfordshire OX20 1TW

Library of Congress Cataloging-in-Publication Data

Lerner, Joshua.
Boulevard of broken dreams : why public efforts to boost entrepreneurship and venture
capital have failed and what to do about it / Josh Lerner.
p. cm. – (The Kauffman Foundation series on innovation and entrepreneurship)
Includes index.
ISBN 978-0-691-14219-7 (hbk. : alk. paper)   1. Entrepreneurship—Government
policy.   2. Venture capital—Government policy.   3. Industrial policy.   I. Title.
HB615.L457 2009
338'.04—dc22
2009025392

British Library Cataloging-in-Publication Data is available

Published in collaboration with the Ewing Marion Kauffman Foundation and
the Berkley Center for Entrepreneurial Studies of New York University

This book has been composed in Electra

Printed on acid-free paper. ∞

press.princeton.edu

Printed in the United States of America

1 3 5 7 9 10 8 6 4 2

CONTENTS

PREFACE AND ACKNOWLEDGMENTS

The origin of this book was a dinner by the Persian Gulf a couple of years ago, on a balmy February evening. My host, alluding to my research on entrepreneurship, asked me what could be said to distill the definitive conclusions emerging from academic publications that could guide the design of a program to promote new businesses. The truthful answer, I had to report, was "Not much."

This conversation brought home to me the gap between academic research and practice in the area of promoting entrepreneurship. This gap has its origins in two unhappy facts:

- First, the academic literature is comparatively sparse: economists have turned only recently to the question of how to boost entrepreneurship. In contrast to other government interventions designed to boost economic growth, such as privatizations, programs to promote entrepreneurship have received little scrutiny by economists. Not only are the theoretical foundations much less well developed, but empirical studies are much fewer in number and generally less sophisticated. While related issues—such as the impact of research and development subsidies[1]—have attracted more attention, definitive answers are scarce even among these better-researched topics.

- Second, the problems are complex: there are no easy answers. In many cases, policymakers face the challenge of having to consider many different policies. It is often unclear how proposed changes will interact with each other. There is no clear "instruction manual" that explains which changes will have the desired effects.

Thus, most conclusions gleaned from the academic literature will necessarily be tentative.

The relative neglect of these matters is very unfortunate. While the sums of money involved in public efforts to promote entrepreneurship are modest compared to public expenditures on defense procurement or retiree benefits, these programs—as we shall see—can profoundly shape the evolution of nations and regions.

These considerations might suggest it would be sensible to delay writing this book until more is known. But policymakers have an urgent need for guidance today. In many cases, these leaders (whether rightly or wrongly) perceive a "window of opportunity," where investments in promoting entrepreneurial activity would be especially fruitful. The economic downturn has both made public interventions into the economy more acceptable and highlighted the poor long-run prospects for many mature industries.

These thoughts suggested the need for a book such as this. Owing to our early stage of understanding, this book is quite different from the traditional article in an academic journal. In particular, it is not an exercise where conclusions can be drawn at the 95 percent confidence level: there is much more ambiguity in many of the conclusions. But while definitive statistical evidence may be lacking for many of its arguments, this book does draw on a blend of evidence: economic theorizing, the limited number of large-sample studies on the topic, case studies, and my own experiences working with national and regional governments struggling to encourage entrepreneurial activity.

This project has had many helpers, to whom I express my gratitude. Excellent research assistance in understanding the historical track records of government programs and summarizing the relevant academic and practitioner literature was provided by Adrian Budischak, Sara Cheche, Yeguang (Shaq) Chi, Catherine Chuter, Kathy Han, Jodi Krawkow, and Yinglan Tan. Chris Allen, as always, was very helpful in assembling statistical data. Financial support for their (and my) work was provided by Harvard Business School's Division of Research. Ralph Lerner and Marianne D'Amico read and commented on several versions of the manuscript. Princeton University Press, as always, was superbly helpful: I thank my editor, Seth Ditchik, as well as Janie Chan and Peter Dougherty.

Three other sources for this work should also be acknowledged. Many of the insights in this book originally emerged from projects for governments in Europe, North America, the Middle East, and Oceania. The chance to work on these projects, and in particular my many helpful conversations with political leaders, economic development officials, entrepreneurs, and venture capitalists, played a key role in shaping these ideas. I would particularly like to thank Colin Gosselin, Abu-Baker Khouri, Jodie Parmar, Stuart Shepherd, and Brian Watson in this regard.

This book also draws on the ideas (and occasionally the words) in my previously published research, including work with Pierre Azoulay, Paul Gompers, Felda Hardymon, Sam Kortum, Ann Leamon, and Antoinette Schoar. I thank them for permission to use here some of our jointly developed ideas, as well as for many conversations that shaped my ideas. I also had helpful conversations with several colleagues, including Ann-Kristin Achleitner, Thomas Hellmann, Peter Henry, and Scott Stern.

Finally, over the past decade, I have had the chance to organize two groups at the National Bureau of Economic Research, devoted to Entrepreneurship and to Innovation Policy and the Economy. The NBER's chief executive officers, Marty Feldstein and Jim Poterba, encouraged these activities. Carl Schramm, Bob Litan, and Bob Strom of the Erwin Marion Kauffman Foundation were generous in supporting these groups. Those settings provided occasions for conversations with friends and colleagues about many of the ideas discussed in this book.

CHAPTER 1

INTRODUCTION

The financial crisis of 2008 opened the door to massive public interventions in the Western economies. In many nations, governments responded to the threats of illiquidity and insolvency by making huge investments in troubled firms, frequently taking large ownership stakes.

The magnitude of these investments boggles the imagination. Consider, for instance, the over $150 billion invested by the U.S. government in AIG (American International Group) in September and November 2008 in exchange for 81 percent of the firm's stock, without any assurances that the ailing insurer would not need more funds. Or the Swiss government's infusion of $60 billion into UBS in exchange for just under 10 percent of the firm's equity: this capital represented about 20 percent of the nation's gross domestic product.[1] Moreover, the pressures in Western nations to rescue other failing sectors—beginning with their automakers—seem unrelenting and suggest that yet more transactions are to come.

Many concerns can be raised about these investments, from the hurried way in which they were designed by a few people behind closed doors to the design flaws that many experts anticipate will limit their effectiveness. But one question has been lost in the discussion. If these extraordinary times call for massive public funds to be used for economic interventions, should they be entirely devoted to propping up troubled entities, or at least partially designed to promote new enterprises? In some sense, 2008 saw the initiation of a massive Western experiment in the government as venture capitalist, but as a very peculiar type of venture capitalist: one that focuses on the most troubled and poorly managed firms in the economy, some of which may be beyond salvation.

Meanwhile, in a different part of the globe, in Dubai, the bitter-sweet fruits of a different type of public intervention can be seen. The emirate experienced truly extraordinary growth in its entrepreneurial environment for much of the past decade. This transformation could be seen through several metrics: new business creation rates, the in-migration of talented and creative individuals from around the region and the world, and the establishment of a regional hub of venture cap-ital, growth equity, and investment banking activity. To cite one, albeit quite noisy, indicator, in the 2007 Global Entrepreneurship Monitor survey, the United Arab Emirates was ranked first among the forty-two countries rated for hosting start-ups geared primarily toward export markets.[2] Among the overall ranking in the number of start-up busi-nesses begun in 2007, the nation moved up to the seventeenth posi-tion from the twenty-ninth spot the year before.

The role of the public sector in effecting this transformation in Dubai is unquestionable.[3] The initial vision for the potential of the government's capital and leadership in transforming the city can be traced back to the 1950s, when the late Sheikh Rashid bin Saeed Al Maktoum dredged the Dubai Creek. The waterway was crucial to Dubai's trading and reexport businesses. (These activities had emerged as the city's primary industries after the collapse of the pearl trade in the aftermath of the Great Depression and the invention of cultured pearls in Japan.) At the time a city of roughly 20,000 residents with few natural resources, Dubai was unable to afford the dredging and expan-sion project itself. To finance the effort, the sheikh essentially had to mortgage the emirate to the emir of Kuwait. Once the dredging work was complete, trading volume promptly increased and Dubai was able to rapidly repay the loan.

This successful project was only the first of a series of investments made by Sheikh Rashid. The most dramatic of these was undoubtedly the decision in 1972 to build a huge new port at Jebel Ali, massive enough to accommodate global shipping vessels, large cruise ships, and aircraft carriers. It was—and remains—the largest port in the re-gion by far. The project, widely seen as hopelessly uneconomic at the time, created one of the world's most successful ports and a key trans-shipment point for trade between the West and China. Numerous

2

other investments followed, such as initiatives to catalyze development of a major airport and the flag carrier Emirates Airlines, hotel and resort projects, and major sporting arenas and events.

Another illustration of this aggressive policy can be seen in the creation of Dubai's Internet City (DIC).[4] This effort was announced in 1999. At the time, technology investment worldwide was booming, and the effort was seen as a way to diversify Dubai's economy from its dependence on the emirate's rapidly dwindling petroleum supply. In addition to developing office space, DIC offered a wide variety of incentives to companies that located there, including tax-free status for corporate earnings (guaranteed for fifty years), exemptions from customs duties, and the right to repatriate profits fully. DIC also offered tenants renewable, fifty-year leases on the land, enabling them to plan long-term projects.

A major focus was on providing amenities in addition to office space. These incentives included computer hardware, such as a world-class network built in collaboration with technology giant Cisco Systems. Many more intangible benefits were provided by DIC as well. These goodies included a three-day incorporation process (which allowed accelerated access to the many legal benefits that firms resident in the center obtained), a simplified immigration process for knowledge workers, help lines to answer any questions the new corporate residents had, and many opportunities for knowledge-sharing and networking among the resident firms. Certain services were geared to entrepreneurial firms, such as the availability of furnished one-room offices for rent on a month-to-month basis, with shared conference space. These services were initially provided by the management of the Internet City itself, and then spun off into an independent company. Throughout, the services were priced at a slight premium in comparison to like facilities, reflecting the particular desirability of this location.

Just as with the Jebel Ali port project, this venture attracted considerable skepticism. The catcalls intensified after the decline in technology and telecommunications stocks in the spring of 2000. But by the time the center opened, a year after being announced, it had attracted about 180 tenants, including major international players in the sector such as Cisco, Hewlett Packard, IBM, Microsoft, Oracle, and Siemens, as well as a variety of start-ups. The cluster continued to grow rapidly in the ensuing years, as many corporations chose the location as a regional hub for their business in the Middle East, Africa, and the Indian subcontinent, and new firms in the region gravitated to the facility.

But public intervention also has its dark side in Dubai, as recent events have revealed. While exact data are hard to come by, numerous analysts suggest that the Dubai government—and its government-linked corporations—is awash in a sea of red ink. In the last decade, public funds appear to have been used more and more indiscriminately for a wide array of highly levered real estate development projects, many of which were "me too" efforts with few broad social benefits or even the promise of attractive private returns.

The consequences of this excessive leverage were apparent in the aftermath of the financial crisis that began in 2008. As construction projects ground to a halt and employers contracted, many recent migrants drifted away in search of greener pastures. The debt incurred from the undisciplined pursuit of growth will be a drag on the emirate in the years to come.[5]

Moreover, in many other parts of the Middle East, governments are facing an even worse outcome: debts from large public expenditures with little new growth to show for their efforts. Numerous governments plowed their newfound oil riches into emulating the Dubai model. But in many cases, instead of seeking to copy the key *principles* behind Dubai's success, they slavishly imitated the same distinct steps that the emirate took, regardless of whether their replication could pass a test of economic logic.

Consider, for instance, the efforts to emulate Dubai by creating regional transport and financial hubs. A plethora of economic analyses have suggested that these businesses have strong network effects, where the dominating position afforded an initial mover with a strong competitive position is very difficult to attack. But rather than identifying and exploiting underserved market opportunities—as Dubai's neighboring emirate, Abu Dhabi, has done with its focus on cultural tourism—far too often the approach of neighboring governments has been to imitate what has worked for Dubai, no matter how modest the chance of repeated success. It is natural to wonder how many viable airport gateways, financial centers, and high-technology hubs can co-exist within a few hundred miles of each other.

This two-sided picture of public investment represents the basic puzzle at work here. When we look at the regions of the world that are, or are emerging as, the great hubs of entrepreneurial activity—places such as Silicon Valley, Singapore, Tel Aviv, Bangalore, and Guangdong and Zhejiang provinces—the stamp of the public sector is unmistakable. Enlightened government intervention played a key role in creating each of these regions. But for each effective government intervention, there have been dozens, even hundreds, of failures, where substantial public expenditures bore no fruit.

This account of the results of public investment might lead the reader to conclude that the pursuit of entrepreneurial growth by the public sector is a massive casino. The public sector is simply making bets, with no guarantees of success. Perhaps there are no lessons to be garnered from the experiences of the successful and the failed efforts to create entrepreneurial hubs.

The truth, however, is very different. In many, many cases, the failure of efforts by governments to promote venture and entrepreneurial activity was completely predictable. These efforts have shared a set of flaws in their design, which doomed them virtually from the start. In many corners of the world, from Europe and the United States to the newest emerging economies, the same classes of problems have reappeared.

The Focus of This Book

Before we plunge into the substance of the book, it is worth highlighting the economic institutions on which we will focus, and mentioning those we won't address.

Fast-growing entrepreneurs have attracted increasing attention both in the popular press and from policymakers. These business creators and the investors who fund them play a dramatic role in creating new industries and revitalizing economies. Many nations have launched efforts to encourage this activity. Such attention is only likely to intensify as nations seek to overcome the deleterious effects of the credit crunch and its recessionary aftereffects. This book is an effort to shed light on the process by which governments can avoid heading down an avenue of false hope, making all too common mistakes in an attempt to stimulate entrepreneurship.

One limitation is that we won't be looking at all efforts to boost entrepreneurship. In recent decades, there has been an explosion in the number of efforts to provide financing and other forms of assistance to the poorest of the world's poor, in order to facilitate their entry into entrepreneurship or the success of the small ventures they already have. Typically, these are "subsistence" businesses, offering services such as snack preparation or clothing repair. Such businesses typically allow the owner and his or her family to get by, but little else. The public policy literature—and indeed academic studies of new ventures—has not always made this distinction between the types of businesses that are being studied.

Our focus here will be exclusively on high-potential new ventures and the policies that enhance them. This choice is not intended to diminish the importance or relevance of efforts to boost microenterprises, but rather reflects the complexity of the field: the dynamics and issues involving micro-firms differ markedly from those associated with their high-potential counterparts. As we'll see, a substantial literature suggests that promising entrepreneurial firms can have a powerful effect in transforming industries and promoting innovation.

It might be obvious to the reader why governments would want to promote entrepreneurship, but why also the frequent emphasis on venture funds as well? The answer lies in the challenges facing many start-up firms, which often require substantial capital. A firm's founder may not have sufficient funds to finance projects alone, and therefore must seek outside financing. Entrepreneurial firms that are characterized by significant intangible assets, expect years of negative earnings, and have uncertain prospects are unlikely to receive bank loans or other debt financing. Venture capital—independently managed, dedicated pools of capital that focus on equity or equity-linked investments in privately held, high-growth companies—can help alleviate these problems.

Typically, venture capitalists do not primarily invest their own capital, but rather raise the bulk of their funds from institutions and individuals. Large institutional investors, such as pension funds and university endowments, want investments in their portfolio that have the potential to generate high yields, such as venture capital, and typically do not mind placing a substantial amount of capital in investments that cannot be liquidated for extended periods. Often, these groups have neither the staff nor the expertise to make such investments themselves. Thus, they invest in partnerships sponsored by venture capital funds, which in turn provide the funds to young firms.

In this book, we'll explore efforts to promote the growth of high-potential entrepreneurial ventures, as well as the venture funds that capitalize them. While the public sector is important in stimulating these activities, I will note that far more often than not, public programs have been failures. Many of these failures could have been avoided, however, if leaders had taken some relatively simple steps in designing and implementing their efforts.

It is also important to note that this book focuses on new ventures, rather than restructurings, leveraged buyouts, and other later-stage private equity investments. Later-stage private equity resembles venture capital in a number of respects, sharing similar legal structures, incentive schemes, and investors. Such equity funds also invest in a type of enterprise that often finds external financing difficult to raise: troubled firms that need to restructure. Like venture capitalists, buyout funds protect the value of their equity stakes by undertaking due diligence before making investments and by retaining powerful oversight rights afterward. The organizations that finance these high-risk, potentially high-reward projects in mature firms pose a different—but quite interesting—set of issues. They are thus the topic for another book!

This book also shies away from the answer to the often-asked question of what makes a good industry for a given nation to promote at a particular time. These questions have, of course, no "one size fits all" answer, but are very specific to the individual circumstances. While the analyses of industrial organization and strategy needed to answer these questions are fascinating, they would take us too far afield.

The Boulevard of Broken Dreams

As I suggested in the preface, our understanding of the ideal policies to promote new ventures is still at an early stage. But the desire for information on how to encourage entrepreneurial activity is very real. Particularly in an era of economic turmoil and recession, governments look to entrepreneurial ventures as economic spark plugs that will reignite growth. This book seeks to address this need, synthesizing approaches that we know work—and warning against those that don't.

The Broad Backdrop

The first three chapters explore why public intervention to boost new venture activity might make sense. If we have heard pronouncements by Silicon Valley patriarchs, we may begin with the view that the government has nothing to contribute to new ventures. Isn't this the realm of heroic entrepreneurs and investors, far removed from pointy-headed government bureaucrats?

In chapter 2, we take an initial look at this issue by reviewing the history of Silicon Valley and several of the pioneering venture capital groups. We find that reality is far more complex than our libertarian entrepreneurial friends might have us believe. In each case we look at, government was an initial catalyst in the growth of the region, sector, or firm.

This is not to minimize that miscues were made along the way. As we'll discuss, a number of challenges faced these entrepreneurs and their investors:

- Silicon Valley's pioneers labored with a "stop and start" pattern of government funding: wartimes would see a surge of funding for research and procurement, which would frequently disappear upon the cessation of hostilities.

- The founders of pioneering venture groups, such as American Research and Development and 3i, did not clearly distinguish in their early years between social goals and financial objectives, which led to a muddled mission and confused investors.

- The Small Business Investment Company was poorly designed initially, with counterproductive requirements, and then implemented inconsistently.

Despite these caveats, it seems clear that the public sector—or in the case of American Research and Development, individuals operating with a broader social framework in mind—proved a critical catalyst to growth in Silicon Valley.

In the third and fourth chapters, we explore the same questions about the role of the public sector, but now in a more systematic manner. We look at the academic literature to explore the arguments for and against government interventions to stimulate entrepreneurship. The third chapter explores the rationales for government investment, which rest on three pillars. First, the role of technological innovation as a spur for economic growth is now widely recognized. Indeed, statements of policy by governments worldwide highlight the importance of innovation in sustaining economic growth and prosperity.

Second, academic research has highlighted the role of entrepreneurship and venture capital in stimulating innovation. Venture financiers and firms have developed tools that are very well suited to the challenging task of nurturing high-risk but promising new ideas. One study estimates that because of these tools, a single dollar of venture capital generates as much innovation as three dollars of traditional corporate research and development. Venture capital and the entrepreneurs it funds will never supplant other wellsprings of innovation, such as vibrant universities and corporate research laboratories (in an ideal world, these components of growth all feed each other). But in an innovative system, a healthy entrepreneurial sector and venture capital industry will be important contributors.

If that were the whole story, the case for public involvement would be pretty compelling. And we probably would not need this book! But the case for public intervention rests as well on a third leg: the argument that *governments* can effectively promote entrepreneurship and venture capital. And as we see in chapter 4, this is a much shakier assumption.

To be sure, entrepreneurial markets have features that allow us to identify a natural role for government in encouraging their evolution. Entrepreneurship is a business in which there are increasing returns. To put the point another way, it is far easier to found a start-up if there are ten other entrepreneurs nearby. In many respects, founders and venture capitalists benefit from their peers. For instance, if entrepreneurs are already active in the market, investors, employees, intermediaries such as lawyers and data providers, and the wider capital markets are likely to be knowledgeable about the venturing process and what strategies, financing, support, and exit mechanisms it requires. In the activities associated with entrepreneurship and venture capital, the actions of any one group are likely to have positive spillovers—or, in the language of economics, "externalities"—for their peers. It is in these types of settings that the government can often play a very positive role as a catalyst.

This observation is supported by numerous examples of government intervention that has triggered the growth of a venture capital sector. For instance, the Small Business Investment Company (SBIC) program in the United States led to the formation of the infrastructure for much of the modern venture capital industry. Many of the early venture capital funds and leading intermediaries in the industry—such as law firms and data providers—began as organizations oriented to the SBIC funds, and then gradually shifted their focus to independent venture capitalists. Similarly, public programs played an important role in triggering the explosive growth of virtually every other major venture market around the globe.

But I also consider in the fourth chapter why there are reasons to be cautious about the efficacy of government intervention. In particular, I highlight two well-documented problems that can derail government programs. First, they can simply get it wrong: allocating funds and support in an inept or, even worse, a counterproductive manner. An extensive literature has examined the factors that affect the quality of governmental efforts in general, and suggests that more competent programs are likelier in nations that are wealthier, with more homogeneous populations, and an English legal tradition.

Economists have also focused on a second problem, delineated in the theory of regulatory capture. These writings suggest that private and public sector entities will organize to capture direct and indirect subsidies that the public sector hands out. For instance, programs geared toward going to nascent entrepreneurs may instead end up boosting cronies of the nation's rulers or legislators. The annals of government venturing programs abound with examples of efforts that have been hijacked in such a manner.

I will discuss examples of both problems in the history of public venturing programs. A few instances are as follows:

- In its haste to roll out the Small Business Investment Company program in the early 1960s, the U.S. Small Business Administration chartered—and funded—hundreds of funds whose managers were incompetent or crooked (chapter 2).

- The incubators taking part in Australia's 1999 BITS (Building on Information Technology Strengths) program frequently captured the lion's share of the subsidies aimed toward entrepreneurs, by forcing the young firms to purchase their own overpriced services (chapter 4).

- Malaysia opened a massive BioValley complex in 2005 with little forethought about whether there would be demand for the facility. The facility soon became known as the "Valley of the Bio-Ghosts" (chapter 6).

- Britain's Labor and Conservative governments subsidized and gave exclusive rights in the 1980s to the biotechnology firm Celltech, whose management team was manifestly incapable of exploiting those resources (chapter 7).

- Norway squandered much of its oil wealth in the 1970s and 1980s propping up failing ventures and funding ill-conceived new businesses begun by relatives of parliamentarians and bureaucrats (chapter 8).

Strategies and Their Limitations

In the fifth through seventh chapters, I look across the policies that governments employ to encourage venture capital and entrepreneurial activity. These take two forms: those that ensure that the economic environment is conducive to entrepreneurial activity and venture capital investments and those that directly invest in companies and funds.

First, it is necessary to ensure that entrepreneurship itself is an attractive option. Often, in their eagerness to get to the "fun stuff" of handing out money, public leaders neglect the importance of setting the table, or creating a favorable environment.

Such efforts to create the right climate for entrepreneurship are likely to have several dimensions. Ensuring that creative ideas can move easily from universities and government laboratories is critically important. However, many entrepreneurs come not from academia, but rather from corporate positions, and studies have documented that, for these individuals, the attractiveness of entrepreneurial activity is very sensitive to tax policy. Also important is ensuring that the law allows firms to enter into the needed contracts—for instance, with a potential financier or a source of technology—and that these contracts can be enforced. Finally, education is likely to be critical. Ensuring that business and technology students are exposed to entrepreneurship classes will allow them to make more informed decisions; and creating training opportunities in entrepreneurship for midcareer professionals is also likely to pay dividends.

Second, it is important to ensure that international investors find the nation or province an attractive one in which to invest. In most of the successful entrepreneurial hubs established in the past two decades, the critical early investments have not been made by domestic institutions, but rather by sophisticated international investors. These investors are likely to have the depth of knowledge and experience that enables them to make substantial bets on the most promising organizations. But these players are likely to be very reluctant to take part if

12

local regulatory conditions are not up to global standards, or if there are substantial doubts about the ability of investors to exit investments. Reaching out to interested and skilled individuals overseas—most often, expatriate entrepreneurs—can also provide a source of capital and expertise.

A final important—though very challenging—role for government is to intervene directly in the entrepreneurial process. As noted above, these programs must be designed thoughtfully, so as to be sensitive to the private sector's needs and to the market's dictates. Because entrepreneurship brings "increasing returns," efforts by governments can play an important role in the industry's early days.

At the same time, governments must avoid the common pitfalls that threaten publicly supported ventures. In the sixth and seventh chapters, I highlight what can go wrong. I divide these pitfalls into two categories: conceptual failings, which doom a program from its very start, and implementation failures, which create problems as the programs enter operation.

One common conceptual failing is to ignore the realities of the entrepreneurial process. For instance, many public venture capital initiatives have been abandoned after a few years: the programs' authors have apparently not understood that these initiatives take many years to bear fruit. Other programs have added requirements—such as the stipulation that portfolio companies focus only on "precommercial" research—that may seem reasonable as public policy but run counter to the nature of the entrepreneurial process. In other cases, reasonable programs have been too tiny to have an impact, or so large that they swamp the already-existing funds.

A second frequently encountered conceptual problem is the creation of programs that ignore the market's dictates. Far too often, government officials have encouraged funding in industries or geographic regions where private interest simply did not exist. Whether these choices have been driven by political considerations or hubris, the result has been wasted resources. Effective programs avoid this problem by demanding that credible private sector players provide matching funds.

If ignored, these broad problems of design can doom a program even before it is started. But plenty of pitfalls remain once programs begin. One common implementation problem is a failure to build in incentives. Far too often, participants in public schemes to promote entrepreneurship do well financially whether or not the program meets objectives. In fact, in many instances, they do well even if the companies go belly-up! The contrast with the best practices among private investors, where scrupulous attention to incentives is commonplace, could not be more striking. Managers of public initiatives must pay attention to various possible scenarios, and avoid incentives, or a lack of incentives, that can lead to problematic behavior.

Another danger in implementation is the failure to design appropriate evaluative mechanisms. Ideally, programs will undergo careful scrutiny at two levels. First, the program itself will be carefully analyzed. While designers should recognize that any initiative will take time to bear fruit, it is important to periodically take stock of which of its aspects appear to work well and which do not. Second, fund managers and firms participating should be scrutinized. It is important to ensure that the groups benefiting from government programs are the most promising in the industry in terms of market performance and can most benefit from public investment, rather than being those most adept at currying favor with the people who are handing out public funds.

A final frequent failing is to ignore the international nature of the entrepreneurial process. Today's venture industry is a global one on many levels. Limited partners' capital commitments, venture capitalists' investments, and entrepreneurial firms' spending increasingly flow across borders and continents. To attempt to build a local entrepreneurial sector and venture capital industry without strong global ties is a recipe for an irrelevant and unsuccessful sector. Yet in many instances, international participation is actively *discouraged*.

A Special Case

In the eighth chapter, we turn to considering a special, but highly visible, manifestation of the government as entrepreneur: the sovereign wealth fund. These institutions have been experiencing remarkable growth, and an even greater increase in scrutiny from business and political leaders worldwide.

14

A sovereign fund can be defined as a state-owned fund that invests in various financial assets. The visibility, diverse goals, and (in many cases) substantial size of these funds mean that managing them is not a simple task.

To be sure, many of the challenges facing sovereign wealth funds are similar to those encountered in the other public venture capital and entrepreneurial promotion schemes that I consider elsewhere in this volume and have already summarized. But these organizations must struggle as well with added issues, which make the effective leadership of sovereign funds especially challenging.

First, these organizations face political scrutiny, particularly in Europe and the United States. One might assume that sovereign funds, which have been part of the economic landscape for more than half a century, are too familiar to cause worry. But the rapid growth of these funds in recent years and their role in a few high-profile transactions have called attention to them and inflamed public anxieties.

Careful scrutiny suggests that many of the criticisms of sovereign funds have been misleading. For instance, many critics have depicted them as concentrating their investments in the most developed nations, while in fact the bulk of their activities have focused on domestic deals and developing nations. At the same time, the sovereign funds—by surrounding themselves with a veil of secrecy, in many cases—have not assuaged anxiety about their role. In this book I argue that greater visibility in funds' objectives and activities could allay some—though probably not all—of this anxiety, but would also impose real costs.

The second major challenge relates to the need to generate good returns on investments. Groups—particularly the larger ones—must struggle with the cruel mathematics of investment management: strategies that may be attractive for a small capital pool become much more difficult to implement with more capital under management. This problem is most acute in alternative investments, such as private equity and real estate, on which many sovereign funds have increasingly focused.

I highlight three responses to this second challenge. First, funds must be creative in choosing their investment classes. Categories that have been successful for previous generations of investors are unlikely to remain lucrative, and it is critical to creatively scan the investment horizon, identifying areas where one can gain a comparative advantage. Second, it is important to realize that building a successful investment program is a major, long-run investment. Identifying and implementing a strategy, and fine-tuning one's approach, cannot be done effectively unless key managers are recruited and retained. Finally, breaking the fund into smaller pieces may yield better returns.

Final Thoughts

This book, then, ends with a nuanced message. To be sure, government has a role in stimulating a vibrant entrepreneurial sector, given the early stage of maturity of entrepreneurial activities in most nations. But at the same time, it is easy for the government to overstep its bounds and squander its investments. Only by designing a program that reflects an understanding of, and a willingness to learn from, the entrepreneurial process can governments be effective.

In particular, I highlight in the final chapter several guidelines for policymakers who want to facilitate entrepreneurship:

- Remember that entrepreneurial activity does not exist in a vacuum: building an environment where new ventures can thrive is a critical first step.

- Leverage the local academic, scientific, and research base effectively.

- Respect the need for conformity to global standards: adopting rules that resemble those found in leading nations will help attract critically important overseas investors.

- Be sure to let the market provide direction when providing subsidies.

- Resist the temptation to "overengineer" public venture initiatives.

- Recognize the long lead times these initiatives require.

16

- Avoid programs that are too small to make a noticeable difference or too big for the market.

- Understand the need for, and actively encourage, strong interconnections with entrepreneurs and investors overseas, rather than focus only on domestic activity.

- Institutionalize careful evaluations of initiatives.

- Realize that the programs to promote entrepreneurship need creativity and flexibility; sometimes they must be refined or killed off.

- Recognize that "agency problems"—when individuals and organizations act to benefit themselves, rather than the broader social good—are universal, and take steps to minimize their danger.

- Make education part of the initiative, including that of overseas investors, local entrepreneurs, and the public sector.

At the same time, there are prescriptions for creating new entrepreneurs that may be seductive, but are best avoided:

- Mandates to local institutional investors to make larger allocations to venture capital, regardless of the nature of the opportunities

- Substantial up-front tax incentives for investments, which can introduce distorted incentives

- A reliance on financial intermediaries to manage these programs, since they are likely to have different incentives

- Matching ill-considered incentives offered by other governments

A CRITICAL CHALLENGE FOR ALL OF US

Programs to boost new ventures might seem like an esoteric corner of public policy, far less important than the big issues of war and peace and health benefits, not to mention the rescue of giant firms that are on the ropes. But this perception can be misleading because of the magnitude of changes that can occur when venture programs are done well.

To understand their importance, we can contrast Jamaica and Singapore.[6] Both are relatively tiny states, with under five million residents apiece. Upon Singapore's independence in 1965—three years after Jamaica's own establishment as a nation—the two nations were about equal in wealth: the gross domestic product (in 2006 U.S. dollars) was $2,850 per person in Jamaica, slightly higher than Singapore's $2,650. Both nations had a centrally located port, a tradition of British colonial rule, and governments with a strong capitalist orientation. (Jamaica, in addition, had plentiful natural resources and a robust tourist industry.) But four decades later, their standing was dramatically different: Singapore had climbed to a per capita GDP of $31,400 (2006 data, in current dollars), while Jamaica's figure was only $4,800.[7]

What accounts for the amazing difference in growth rates? There are many explanations: soon after independence, Singapore aggressively invested in infrastructure such as its port, subsidized its system of education, maintained an open and corruption-free economy, and established sovereign wealth funds that made a wide variety of investments. It has also benefited from a strategic position on the key sea lanes heading to and from East Asia. Jamaica, meanwhile, spent many years mired in political instability, particularly the disastrous administration of Michael Manley during the 1970s. Dramatic shifts from a market economy to a socialist orientation and back again, with the attendant inflation, economic instability, crippling public debt, and violence, made the development and implementation of a consistent long-run economic policy difficult.

In explaining Singapore's economic growth, it is hard not to give considerable credit to its policies toward entrepreneurship. As we'll discuss in more detail below, the government has experimented with a wide variety of efforts to develop an entrepreneurial sector:

- The provision of public funds for venture investors seeking to locate in the city-state
- Subsidies for firms in targeted technologies

- Encouragement of potential entrepreneurs and mentoring for fledgling ventures

- Subsidies for leading biotechnology researchers to move their laboratories to Singapore

- Awards for failed entrepreneurs (with a hope of encouraging risk-taking)

While much of the initial growth in Singapore can be attributed to sound macroeconomic policies, political stability, and various other factors, the nation's entrepreneurship initiatives have played an increasingly important role in stimulating growth.

The contrast with Jamaica is striking. Jamaica has long had a high rate of subsistence entrepreneurship: for instance, the 2006 Global Entrepreneurship Monitor survey placed it among the highest of the forty-two nations it examined in various rates of entrepreneurial activity.[8] Yet other data collected by the Monitor—and corroborated in anecdotal accounts—suggests that early-stage entrepreneurship is translated into full-fledged business activity at a very low rate. On this measure, the island nation ranked among the lowest nations (twenty-eighth among the thirty-five countries ranked by GEM in 2005).[9]

Some of the reasons for the inability of Jamaican entrepreneurs to grow can be seen in the World Bank's reports on the barriers to entrepreneurs. The "Doing Business" series assesses, across 178 countries, the obstacles faced by an entrepreneur in performing various standardized tasks (thereby avoiding some of the subjectivity associated with other attempts to rank entrepreneurship).

In several critical indicators, Jamaica ranked extremely low in the World Bank's 2008 analysis.[10] These suggest some of the barriers that hold back the growth of entrepreneurial enterprises:

- Of the 178 countries studied, Jamaica ranked 170th in the burden of complying with tax regulations. The ranking reflects not just the cost of the taxes themselves, but also the administrative burdens associated with complying with the tax code. The World Bank's analysis suggests that the total cost of complying with all tax laws in Jamaica amounts to just over one-half of gross profits for the typical entrepreneur. Numerous studies have suggested that one of the most important sources of financing for the typical entrepreneur is cash flow generated by the business itself, which is plowed back into the business. If so much of entrepreneurs' income is going to meet tax obligations, business owners are unlikely to have the resources to invest in their enterprises. By way of contrast, Singapore ranked second worldwide, with a burden of just 23 percent.[11]

- Similarly, when the cost of registering property is compared, Jamaica ranked 108th out of 178: the cost of registering property was equal to 13.5 percent of the value of the property. (By comparison, the ratio in the United States is 0.5 percent of the value.)[12] The high cost of registering property means that fewer people register their holdings, which in turn leads to less secure property rights. Most critically, entrepreneurs who do not hold a firm legal title to property are unlikely to be able to borrow against this holding from a bank. Once again, this comparison suggests that entrepreneurs have fewer resources for growing their enterprises.

One of the most visible manifestations of this lack of activity may be in Jamaica's productivity: from 1973 to 2007, the nation actually experienced *negative* productivity growth.[13] Making this poor performance even more striking is the fact that during this period the developed nations experienced substantial growth through the implementation of information technology, and many developing markets experienced even faster growth as they caught up with technologies adopted earlier in the West.

This disparity may change in future years: Jamaica enjoyed a surge in income with the rise of energy and commodity prices, and the most recent prime ministers have shown a greater awareness of, and willingness to lower, barriers to entrepreneurship. But the disparate experiences of Singapore and Jamaica over the past four decades demonstrate why all of us should care about entrepreneurship.

The promotion of business ventures is of critical importance to all of us. While the challenges facing government initiatives may seem arcane and technical, well-considered policies are likely to profoundly influence our opportunities, as well as those of our children and grandchildren. Misguided policies, unfortunately, will also help determine the future. However challenging the encouragement of entrepreneurship may seem, it is truly too important to be left to the policy specialists!

PART ONE

CAN BUREAUCRATS HELP ENTREPRENEURS?

CHAPTER 2

A LOOK BACKWARDS

Before exploring *how* governments can help entrepreneurs, it is important to understand *if* they can be effective at all. In the next three chapters, we will explore the major justifications for public intervention to promote entrepreneurship and venture capital. We'll begin by posing questions that doubtless will be in the back of many readers' minds: most pressingly, how can we reasonably expect government officials to help freewheeling entrepreneurs and venture investors?

In this chapter, we'll seek to answer this question by exploring a few episodes from the history of entrepreneurship. By examining the history of pioneering entrepreneurial regions and venture funds, we'll see that they are not just creations of "capitalist cowboys" chasing profits. In each case, there were many parents, including government agencies and public-spirited citizens with a broad set of goals. Together, these stories suggest that a skeptical doubt that government has any role in promoting entrepreneurship is too simple.

A SKEPTIC'S QUERIES

The skeptic might well wonder why there is a need for government encouragement for entrepreneurship and venture capital. During the past three decades, there has been a tremendous boom in the economic role of high-growth entrepreneurial firms and the venture capitalists who fund them.

This growth is seen most dramatically among venture funds, since they are tracked more carefully than entrepreneurial ventures. The pool of U.S. venture capital funds grew from about $1 billion in 1980

Investment Amount (in 2007 US$ billion)

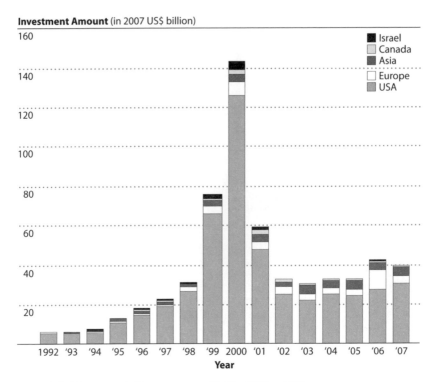

Figure 2.1. Venture capital investment worldwide, 1992 to 2007

to about $100 billion in 2008. Venture capital's growth over that period has outstripped that of almost every class of financial product (one exception is its close cousin, buyout funds, which have grown even faster). This is captured in figure 2.1, which shows the growth of venture activity worldwide.[1]

Moreover, where such funds are located is also becoming more diverse and global. Venture capital was originally concentrated almost exclusively in a few small corners of the developed world, such as Silicon Valley, the western suburbs of Boston, and around Cambridge University in England. The venture industry in 1996, as figure 2.2 illustrates, was very much dominated by activity in the United States.[2] The same was true of most years before and since. In recent years, however, venturing activity has become far more global. While the United States still captured the lion's share of funding, by 2007 the

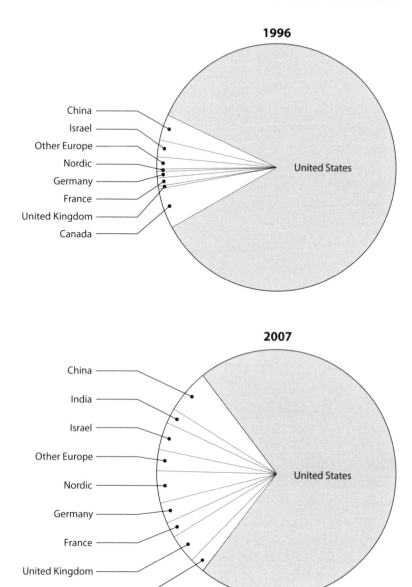

Figure 2.2. Geographic distribution of venture capital, 1996 and 2007

share of funding heading to Asia—especially China and India—and other markets from Toronto to Tel Aviv was growing rapidly.

These data reflect the increasingly global focus of entrepreneurial activity. Through the 1990s, many venture capital funds—particularly those in Silicon Valley—had an extremely parochial view, wishing only to invest in firms within a few miles of their office. Attitudes have changed dramatically in recent years, as groups have taken increasingly global perspectives. Steps taken include increasing the share of investments outside their native countries or regions, creating overseas funds in addition to their domestic ones, and forming strategic partnerships with non-U.S. groups.

Moreover, scientists and engineers, who in the 1990s saw in the United States their only opportunity to pursue a cutting-edge start-up, are increasingly involved in ventures in their native lands as financiers, advisors, or on-the-ground entrepreneurs. Expatriates are important sources of new ideas and capital for ventures: for instance, a surge of Indian-born entrepreneurs doing research in semiconductors in the United States is likely to lead to a boom a few years later in similar ventures in India.[3]

A more subtle reason for being skeptical of the need for public intervention lies in the variations in figure 2.1. The sector has been characterized by a pattern of boom and bust: the rapid increases in fund-raising in the mid-1980s and late 1990s were followed by precipitous declines in, respectively, the early 1990s and early 2000s. Indeed, if our data took us back that far, we'd probably see the same patterns on a smaller scale in the 1950s and 1960s! In many cases, groups raised huge amounts of capital that they invested foolishly, either funding entrepreneurs who never should have raised capital in the first place, or else giving far too much money to promising entrepreneurs.

This instability has been part and parcel of the funding of new ventures. For instance, during the 1980s venture capitalists backed many of the most successful high-technology companies, including Cisco Systems, Genentech, Microsoft, and Sun Microsystems. But the industry did not present a picture of smooth growth: commitments to the venture capital industry during this decade were very uneven. The annual flow of money into venture capital funds increased by a factor of

Returns (percent)

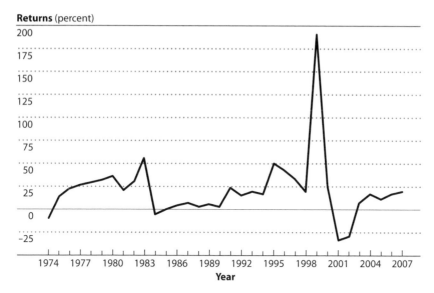

Figure 2.3. U.S. venture capital returns, 1974 to 2007

ten during the first half of the 1980s, but steadily declined from 1987 through 1991 as investors grew disappointed with the sector.

Much of this pattern of excitement and disillusionment was driven by the changing fortunes of venture capital investments. Returns on venture capital funds declined sharply in the mid-1980s after being exceedingly attractive in the 1970s. (See figure 2.3 for returns from U.S. venture funds over these years.)[4] This fall was apparently triggered by overinvestment in a few industries, such as computer hardware, and the entry of many inexperienced venture capitalists. The same cycle was seen among the pioneering funds geared toward European and Japanese entrepreneurs over the same period.

The 1990s saw these patterns repeated on an unprecedented scale. Much of the decade saw dramatic growth and excellent returns in almost every part of the venture capital industry. This recovery was triggered by several factors. The exit of many inexperienced investors at the beginning of the decade meant that the remaining groups faced less competition for transactions. The healthy market for the initial public offerings during much of the decade meant that it was easier

29

for all investors to exit venture capital transactions. Meanwhile, the extent of technological innovation—particularly in industries related to information technology—created extraordinary opportunities for venture capitalists. New capital commitments to venture funds rose in response to these changing circumstances, increasing to record levels by the year 2000.

But as had often happened before, venture activity increased at a pace that was unsustainable. Institutional and individual investors—attracted by the tremendous returns enjoyed by venture funds—poured money into the industry at unprecedented rates. In many cases, groups staggered under the weight of capital. In other cases, groups that should have not raised capital garnered considerable funds.

Too rapid growth led to overstretched partners, inadequate due diligence, and, in many cases, poor investment decisions. Thus, we saw such scenes as venture capitalists driving around Silicon Valley, handing out checks after printing up deal documents in their car trunks. The behavior of entrepreneurs was even less restrained: think of Internet entrepreneurs in the late 1990s throwing Christmas parties with Cristal champagne, buying impossible-to-understand advertisements on the Super Bowl for many millions of dollars, and moving into extravagant marble-clad offices.[5]

While the pattern seen in figure 2.1 was largely driven by activity in the United States and western Europe, the dramatic boom and bust of investment is certainly not unique to the developed world. Figure 2.4 shows the level of venture capital and growth equity investment in China and Hong Kong.[6] Here again, we see the same ebb and flow (similar patterns could be seen in many other markets, from Latin America to eastern Europe).

And this brings us back to the public sector. In an ideal world, we might think, public investors would even out these variations, encouraging investments at times when there are few, and stepping back when the market overheats. But given the tendency of some politicians to jump on the bandwagon at exactly the moment it careens off the road, can we trust them here? We can reasonably worry that gov-

Investment Amount (in 2007 US$ billion)

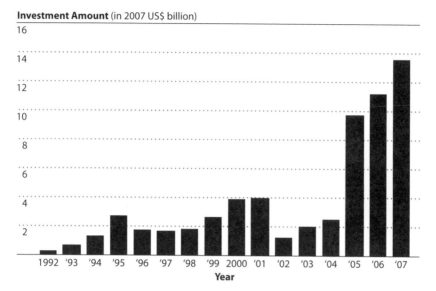

Figure 2.4. China and Hong Kong private equity activity, 1992 to 2007

ernment officials will only worsen this boom-and-bust pattern, by throwing money at these ventures at precisely the wrong times.

Consider some past examples, such as the Chinese venture market.[7] The boom in the late 1990s and early 2000s was largely fueled by investors in the United States and western Europe, who were attracted to the tremendous growth potential of the Chinese market despite the immaturity of the sector and lack of experienced venture professionals. As the money flowed in, the market came under many strains, including rising valuations. Many of the groups that had raised overseas money were unable to maintain a disciplined focus: for instance, Chengwei Ventures made ten investments in its first year of operation, often in very young Internet companies, despite having marketed itself to investors as undertaking extensive due diligence and having a hands-on approach to investing.[8]

Given this period's tremendous increase in activity—and the associated growing pains—one might expect the public sector to see little need to stimulate investment. But a wide variety of state-related entities,

31

from provincial and municipal governments to state-owned enterprises, launched venture initiatives around this time. While a few groups backed with public funds, such as New Margin (funded by the Shanghai municipal government), proved to be enduring successes, the vast majority were unsuccessful. Public funds simply poured fuel on the fire, overheating this rapidly growing market. Again, the role of the public sector in stimulating venture activity raises troubling questions.

The (Uncensored) Story of Silicon Valley

However compelling the skeptical questions delineated above may appear, they are too simple. In this chapter, we will consider the historical record and what it tells us about the role of government in stimulating venture activity.

The limitations of the skeptic's view can perhaps best be illustrated through the story of Silicon Valley. This example may seem surprising, as it might be thought that the role of the public sector was minimal here—that it was the rugged individualism of entrepreneurs and venture capitalists that established the region.

Certainly, this is the story that many Silicon Valley luminaries love to tell. T. J. Rodgers, the colorful founder of Cyprus Semiconductor, has stated, "Silicon Valley is an island of freedom and free markets, more in line with 1776 America and its laissez faire government than with America [today] and its interventionist government. . . . I do not want more government in Silicon Valley. Government can do only two things here: take our money, limiting our economic resources; or pass laws, limiting our other freedoms."[9] But the reality is a bit more complex, as a brief history of Silicon Valley reveals.[10]

Many narratives of the history of Silicon Valley begin with 1955, when William Shockley founded Shockley Transistor in Palo Alto, which would soon in turn spawn Fairchild Semiconductor and much of the modern semiconductor industry. Other accounts extend back to 1938, when Frederick Terman, dean of Stanford's Engineering School, encouraged (and indeed, directly assisted in financing) his students William Hewlett and David Packard to found Hewlett-Packard. The powerful culture that drove Silicon Valley during its growth over the past few decades—with close ties between local universities and start-up firms, the absence of legal or social barriers to job-switching, an active venture community to finance new entities, and a willingness to work with young firms—has also been rightly celebrated by Annalee Saxenien and other authors.

At the same time, it is important to note that the story of Silicon Valley's creation is more complex than many of these accounts, which often rest upon what Timothy Sturgeon calls "the myth of 'instant industrialization.'"[11] In particular, a review of the histories of Silicon Valley suggests two facts that are little appreciated. First, the culture of, and approach to, doing business in Silicon Valley was profoundly shaped by the pioneering firms in the early decades of the twentieth century. Second, the public sector, especially the U.S. Department of Defense, played a crucial role in accelerating the early growth of the region.

The first point can be illustrated by the early history of Silicon Valley. As documented by Sturgeon, the first three decades of the twentieth century saw a series of pioneering technology firms in the Bay Area. These included Federal Telegraph Company, Magnavox, Fisher Research, Litton Engineering Research, and Heintz & Kaufman. While the level of activity was modest relative to contemporary ventures in the eastern United States, these entities established the template that other groups would follow in decades to come. Among the elements that would be commonplace in subsequent years were the following:

- The active involvement of Stanford University as a source of technology and funding. Cyril Elwell, a Stanford graduate, raised initial financing for Federal Telegraph in 1909 with the help of Stanford's president and the head of its civil engineering department, and later made extensive use of the Stanford High Voltage Laboratory.[12] In the 1930s, Frederick Terman would play a key role in nurturing Hewlett-Packard and Litton Engineering.[13]

- The proliferation of spin-offs. Federal Telegraph produced a number of new firms, when employees left to pursue seemingly tangential technologies or explore new markets. As early as the formation of Magnavox's speaker business in 1910, this form of company creation, which would become part and parcel of the Silicon Valley way of doing business,[14] was established. Metal detector manufacturer Fisher Research and Litton Engineering Laboratories (which began as a vacuum tube manufacturer before evolving into Litton Industries) were two other Federal Telegraph spin-offs during the interwar years.[15]

- The reliance on local financiers for capital. While the formal venture industry was several decades away from forming in California, wealthy angel investors such as William Crocker and Henry Mc-Micking played an important role in financing firms.[16]

The second point is that, especially during these early years, the government played a critical role in shaping Silicon Valley. Many of these pioneering firms relied on military contracts to get established and grow. Examples of firms and activities that benefited materially include Federal Telegraph and Magnavox during World War I and the years thereafter; Ralph Heinze's pioneering work on airplane-based power systems between the world wars; Dalmo-Victor, Hewlett-Packard, and Litton Engineering during World War II; and Varian Associates during the Korean War.

The success that Silicon Valley firms experienced during wartimes reflected several factors. First, in light of the dominant patent portfolios that incumbent firms (especially RCA) had assembled in civilian technologies (such as radio), Silicon Valley firms tended to focus instead on military electronics and advanced electronic instruments. Second, geographical circumstance was an important factor, especially during the critical years of World War II. Santa Clara County (the epicenter of what would become Silicon Valley) was convenient to major defense facilities and manufacturers in Oakland, Richmond, and San Francisco; and, of course, its proximity to the Pacific Ocean was helpful in light of the focus on fighting the Japanese.[17]

It should be acknowledged that this federal funding was a mixed blessing. Typically, funding for research and orders would grow rapidly during wartime, only to be abruptly cut upon the end of hostilities: hardly ideal for managing a growing firm. The more successful firms in the region were able to reinvent themselves during the times of these cutbacks; others languished or were sold.

Despite these limitations, Terman continued to focus on military markets in the years after World War II. In particular, he argued that the share of federal contracts going to Stanford and Bay Area businesses was unfairly low, given the level of technical sophistication and the production of engineering Ph.D.s. Stanford helped address this deficiency by establishing the Stanford Research Institute, whose goal was to conduct defense-related research and assist local businesses to break into these markets. Indeed, many of the pioneering firms of the "modern" Silicon Valley, such as Fairchild Semiconductor, relied on government contracts for much of their initial growth.[18]

These comments are not meant to minimize other creative endeavors that Terman and his contemporaries pursued and that helped put Silicon Valley on the map. The attraction to the Stanford campus of select teams of scientists pursuing highly visible, cutting-edge technologies, the creation of an industrial park nearby the university, and the encouragement of cooperative programs where students could work with cutting-edge local firms all boosted the region and its stature.

Despite these examples of private initiatives, it is important to note that the world Rodgers describes is unrealistically simplistic. The public sector did play a key role in shaping the evolution of Silicon Valley, particularly in its earlier years. The impact of public funding, to be sure, was considerably less during the years of spectacular growth, the late 1970s and the 1980s. But in many senses, federal money played a crucial role when it mattered most: during the period when the foundation for that spectacular growth was being built and key aspects of the Silicon Valley business culture were being developed and refined.

The Birth of Venture Capital

Not only was the formation of the entrepreneurial cluster of Silicon Valley driven in key respects by public sector intervention, but so too was the venture capital industry itself.

35

Of course, fast-growing firms were able to raise financing before the creation of the venture industry. Banks provided debt in the form of loans, and for more long-run, riskier investments, wealthy individuals provided equity. By the last decades of the nineteenth century and the first decades of the twentieth century, wealthy families had established offices to manage their investments. Families such as the Phippes, Rockefellers, Vanderbilts, and Whitneys invested in and advised a variety of business enterprises, including the predecessor entities to AT&T, Eastern Airlines, and McDonnell Douglas.

But by the time of the Great Depression of the 1930s, there was a widespread perception that the existing ways of financing fast-growing young firms were inadequate.[19] Not only were many promising companies going unfunded, but investors with high net worth frequently did not have the time or skills to work with young firms to address glaring management deficiencies. Nor were the alternatives set up by the Roosevelt administration during the New Deal—such as the Reconstruction Finance Corporation—seen as satisfactory. The rigidity of the loan evaluation criteria, the extensive red-tape associated with the award process, and the fears of political interference and regulations all suggested a need for an alternative.

The first formal venture capital firm was thus established with a broader set of goals in mind than just making money.[20] American Research and Development (ARD) grew out of the concerns that the United States, having been pushed out of the depression by the stimulus of wartime spending by the federal government, would soon revert to economic lethargy when the war ended. In October 1945, Ralph Flanders, then head of the Federal Reserve Bank of Boston, argued that if this danger was to be addressed, a new enterprise was needed, with the goal of financing new businesses. He argued that the enterprise would not only need to be far more systematic in "selecting the most attractive possibilities and spreading the risk" than most individual investors had been, but would need to tap into the nation's "great accumulation of fiduciary funds" (i.e., pension funds and other institutional capital) if it was to be successful in the long term.[21]

ARD was formed a year later to try to realize this vision. Flanders recruited a number of civic and business leaders to join in the effort, including MIT president Karl Compton. But the day-to-day management of the fund fell on the shoulders of Harvard Business School professor Georges F. Doriot. ARD in its communications emphasized that its goal was to fund and aid new companies in order to generate "an increased standard of living for the American people." While profitability was a goal of the effort, in the words of Pat Liles, financial returns "were not the overriding purpose of the firms. Instead, they were depicted as a necessary part of the process."[22]

This tension between the broader social goals and financial returns ran through ARD's first two decades. In part, these dual goals reflected the tensions inherent in being a public company. Despite Flanders's emphasis on institutional capital, because of limited interest ARD had been able to raise its initial $5 million only by completing a public offering. (The first venture capital limited partnership, Draper, Gaither, and Anderson, was not formed until 1958.) Many of the investors—perhaps having been persuaded by overzealous brokers to buy the shares—had not appreciated the extended time period that it would take to realize capital gains or other profits from the early-stage companies that dominated ARD's portfolio. Doriot, as a result, spent much of the 1950s and 1960s defending the longer-run objectives of the fund. In *Fortune's* rather unsympathetic portrait of ARD in 1967, Doriot was quoted: "Your sophisticated shareholders make five points and then sell out. But we have our hearts in our companies, we are really doctors of childhood diseases here. When bankers or brokers tell me I should sell an ailing company, I ask them, 'Would you sell a child running a temperature of 104?'"[23]

The same tension underlay the next great experiment to promote venture activity, the Small Business Investment Companies (SBICs). These federally guaranteed risk-capital pools proliferated during the 1960s, and accounted for the bulk of all venture capital raised during these years.[24]

The rationale for these entities was similar to that invoked by Doriot: numerous promising entrepreneurs were unable to garner the capital needed to commercialize their ideas. But in one important respect the SBICs were unlike the pioneering efforts of the 1930s: legislators realized that government bureaucrats—no matter how well intentioned—

were probably not the right people to make the tricky decisions about which businesses to fund. Instead, this responsibility would be put in the hands of the private sector.

As enacted in 1958, the SBICs received two powerful mandates: they could borrow up to half their capital from the federal government and would also receive a variety of favorable tax incentives. In return, the SBICs had to confine themselves to investing in small businesses. More onerously, the investments were limited to those structured in certain ways: for instance, the SBICs could not hold equity in firms (though the debt could be convertible to equity), and their control over these firms was also restricted. Moreover, steps that seem like second nature to venture capitalists—such as offering stock options to employees of the firms—were sharply restricted.

These features of the SBIC program were criticized by knowledgeable observers even before the legislation enabling the funds was enacted. The criticism of the program intensified in the early 1960s, when a large number of SBICs were financed, often with minimal review. The entities receiving charters and loans from the government included some run by inexperienced financiers who undertook lines of business very different from those originally intended by Congress—such as real estate development—and corrupt funds determined to make "sweetheart" financings to dubious businesses run by friends, relatives, and, in a few cases, organized crime. Nine out of ten SBICs violated federal regulations in some way.[25] The SBIC program consequently drew extensive congressional criticism for low financial returns and for fraud and waste. Despite some wavering, the officials responsible for the program (and the executive branch more generally) remained committed to it and resisted calls to dismantle it.

Viewed with the benefit of hindsight, however, the legacy of the program from the 1950s and 1960s looks quite different. Though few of today's significant funds began as a part of the SBIC program, it did stimulate the proliferation of many venture-minded institutions in Silicon Valley and Route 128, the nation's two major nurseries of entrepreneurs. These institutions included law firms and accounting groups geared specifically to the needs of entrepreneurial firms. For example,

Venture Economics, which originated as the SBIC Reporting Service in 1961, gradually expanded its scope to become the major source of returns data on the entire venture industry. Moreover, some of the United States' most dynamic technology companies—including Apple Computer, Compaq (now part of Hewlett-Packard), and Intel—received support from the SBIC program before they went public. Similar lessons could be drawn from programs modeled after the SBIC program in other nations such as China and Singapore.

This applause for the catalytic role of the SBIC program, however, is not meant to suggest that it remains a useful program.[26] Like far too many public entrepreneurship and venture capital programs, it has proven virtually impossible to "kill off." It continues despite the fantastic growth of venture capital in recent decades and ample evidence that the bureaucratic rules associated with the program have scared off most talented venture capitalists. (For instance, arcane rules govern the type of securities that can be used by the venture funds participating in the program, the extent to which they can give follow-on financings to firms in their portfolios, and their holding periods.) Moreover, the consequences of the program remain remarkably unexamined, despite the considerable amount of funds that have gone into the effort over the years. The Specialized SBIC program, which is geared toward minority businesses, proved almost impossible even to modify, notwithstanding the extremely high failure rate of funds in that program's first three decades.[27] In chapter 7, we'll talk about how this failure to seriously review the program runs counter to best practices.

Even the dramatic growth of the venture industry in the late 1970s and early 1980s can be attributed in large part to the public sector. Much of the shift was owing to the U.S. Department of Labor's clarification of the Employee Retirement Income Security Act's "prudent man" rule in 1979. Prior to that year, legislation restrained pension funds from investing substantial amounts of money in venture capital or other high-risk asset classes. The Department of Labor's clarification of the rule explicitly allowed pension managers to invest in high-risk assets, including venture capital. Numerous specialized funds—

concentrating in such areas as leveraged buyouts and mezzanine transactions and such hybrids as venture leasing—sprang up during these years.

The same pattern, where government intervention played a crucial role, was repeated in many other nations, from Germany to India. Consider, for instance, 3i Group plc, one of the oldest private equity groups in Europe.[28] Its most direct predecessor, the Industrial and Commercial Finance Corporation (ICFC), was founded in 1945 by political and financial leaders to provide long-term capital for small and medium-sized firms, to help domestic industry recover from the ravages of World War II and the Great Depression that had preceded it. The Bank of England and the five major clearing banks at the time funded the effort with £10 million in equity ownership, in effect establishing a future competitor.

ICFC initially used both debt and equity to fulfill its mandate. This was a tricky proposition, as assessing the long-term prospects of small private businesses was not a widely held skill. Operating among small to medium-sized businesses that were often family-owned and had little history of external funding, the new organization had to invent not just itself, but also an entire skill set.

Under Lord William Piercy, its first chairman, ICFC became somewhat of a financial maverick and an innovator, working across much of the economy and injecting a new measure of competition into London's financial circles. For instance, in the early 1950s, ICFC significantly undercut the prevailing fees charged to underwrite stock issues for medium-sized companies. Despite the controversy this pricing generated, the organization developed a substantial underwriting business during that decade, even as the market rate for such services dropped by half. By the mid-1990s, having largely transformed the investment banking market, 3i had essentially ceased underwriting.

ICFC helped create a greater awareness of the power and usefulness of equity for small companies, especially those that were family-owned. Starting in 1950, ICFC saw the chance to drive growth by expanding into regions outside London, moving first into Birmingham and then, by 1953, into Manchester and Edinburgh. The local offices were encouraged to make independent investment decisions, but also bore re-

sponsibility for them. This expanding branch network (twenty-nine offices by 1972) and devolved decision-making contrasted with the
clearing banks' strategy of centralized decision-making and reduced
attention to small regional businesses.

Over the years, the firm (renamed 3i) expanded the classes of investments it made—for instance, moving into buyouts and early-stage venture capital. It backed a number of companies that became significant
successes, including Bond Helicopters, Caledonian Airways (later
British Caledonian), and Oxford Instruments, the pioneer of magnetic
resonance imaging (MRI).

Over the years, 3i's dominant position as the primary provider of equity capital to private British businesses eroded. Additional venture
capital and private equity groups entered the market, in a number of
cases (for instance, Apax and Permira) experiencing growth that far
outstripped that of 3i. Meanwhile, 3i transformed itself, in some ways
increasingly resembling other venture groups (i.e., dropping some of
the far-flung product lines, like consulting and ship financing) and in
other ways, becoming more peculiar (going public on the London
Stock Exchange). But it remains an enduring financier of private firms
of different degrees of development. The bottom line is clear: not only
did public intervention establish a viable investor in 3i, but it established a template that many other firms, operating without the benefits
of public financing, were able to follow.

Wrapping Up

I began this chapter by giving voice to a skeptic, who wondered about
the likelihood that government intervention could make a difference.
But the historical episodes reviewed here suggested a more complex
picture.

In particular, we saw that Silicon Valley was far from a creation of
unfettered capitalism. Rather, public subsidies—particularly during
the two world wars—catalyzed its growth and shaped its critical features. Similarly, the pioneering firms in the venture industry were initially shaped largely by government interventions and public-spirited

41

citizens. While government invention wasn't the entire story, it provided an important spur.

Moreover, these experiences are the rule rather than the exception. As noted in the introduction, virtually every hub of cutting-edge entrepreneurial activity in the world today had its origins in proactive government intervention. Similarly, the venture capital industry in many nations has been profoundly shaped by government intervention.

In the next two chapters, we'll look at systematic arguments explaining why government has an important role to play in the development of entrepreneurship. As we'll see, there's a considerable rationale for public intervention. But important cautions must also be raised.

CHAPTER 3

WHY SHOULD POLICYMAKERS CARE?

At this point we are familiar with the argument that government has no role in promoting venture capital and entrepreneurship. In the last chapter, we looked at some historical evidence that planted seeds of doubt about this argument. Now we'll turn to more systematic evidence, as articulated in recent research.

The case that policymakers should indeed care about new ventures and venture capitalists—and do have a role to play in facilitating their activity—rests on three foundations. The bulk of this chapter reviews the first two critical rationales: that innovation is critical to growth, and that new ventures can stimulate innovation. As we'll see, both rationales are quite compelling. We'll discuss the third critical link in the argument in chapter 4.

INNOVATION IS LINKED TO GROWTH

Since the 1950s, economists have understood that innovation is critical to economic growth. Our lives are more comfortable and longer than those of our great-grandparents on many dimensions. To cite just three improvements: antibiotics cure once-fatal infections, long-distance communications cost far less, and the burden of household chores is greatly reduced. At the heart of these changes has been the progress of technology and business.

Economists have documented the strong connection between technological progress and economic prosperity, both across nations and over time. This insight grew out of studies done by the pioneering student of technological change, Morris Abramowitz.[1] He realized that there are ultimately only two ways of increasing the output of the economy: (1) increasing the number of inputs that go into the productive process (e.g., by having workers stay employed until the age of sixty-seven, instead of retiring at sixty-two), or (2) developing new ways to get more output from the same inputs. Abramowitz measured the growth in the output of the American economy between 1870 and 1950—the amount of material goods and services produced—and then computed the increase in inputs (especially labor and financial capital) over the same time period. To be sure, this was an imprecise exercise: he needed to make assumptions about the growth in the economic impact of these input measures. After undertaking this analysis, he discovered that growth of inputs between 1870 and 1950 could account only for about 15 percent of the actual growth in the output of the economy. The remaining 85 percent could not be explained through the growth of inputs. Instead, the increased economic activity stemmed from innovations in getting more stuff from the same inputs.

Other economists in the late 1950s and 1960s undertook similar exercises. These studies differed in methodologies, economic sectors, and time periods, but the results were similar. Most notably, Robert Solow, who later won a Nobel Prize for this work, identified an almost identical "residual" of about 85 percent.[2] The results were so striking because most economists for the previous 200 years had been building models in which economic growth was treated as if it was primarily a matter of adding more inputs: if you just had more people and dollars, more output would invariably result.

Instead, these studies suggested, the crucial driver of growth was changes in the ways inputs were used. The magnitude of this unexplained growth, and the fact that it was exposed by researchers using widely divergent methodologies, persuaded most economists that innovation was a major force in the growth of output.

In the decades since the 1950s, economists and policymakers have documented the relationship between innovation—whether new scientific discoveries or incremental changes in the way that factories and service businesses work—and increases in economic prosperity. Not just identifying an unexplained "residual," studies have documented the positive effects of technological progress in areas such as information technology. Thus, an essential question for the economic future of a country is not only what it produces, but how it goes about producing it.

This relationship between innovation and growth has been recognized by many governments. From the European Union—which has targeted increasing research spending as a key goal in the next few years—to emerging economies such as China, leaders have embraced the notion that innovation is critical to growth.

NEW VENTURES SPUR INNOVATION

The second underpinning of the argument for government support of entrepreneurship stems from the insight that new firms are particularly innovative.

The Size, Age, and Innovation of Firms

Initially, economists generally overlooked the creative power of new firms: they suspected that the bulk of innovations would stem from large industrialized concerns. For instance, Joseph Schumpeter, one of the pioneers of the serious study of entrepreneurship, posited that large firms had an inherent advantage in innovation relative to smaller enterprises.

But these initial beliefs have not stood the test of time: indeed, today, such suggestions look like the intellectual by-product of an era that saw large firms and their industrial laboratories (such as IBM and AT&T) replace the independent inventors who accounted for a large part of innovative activity in the late nineteenth and early twentieth centuries.

In today's world, Schumpeter's hypothesis of large-firm superiority does not accord with casual observation. In numerous industries, such as medical devices, communication technologies, semiconductors, and software, leadership is in the hands of relatively young firms whose growth was largely financed by venture capitalists and public equity markets. (Think, for example, of Boston Scientific, Cisco, Intel, and Microsoft.) Even in industries where established firms have retained dominant positions, such as finance, small firms have developed an increasing share of the new ideas, and then licensed or sold them to larger concerns.

This pattern, new ventures playing a key role in stimulating innovation, has been particularly pronounced in the past decade. The two arenas that have seen perhaps the most potentially revolutionary technological innovation—biotechnology and the Internet—were driven by smaller entrants. Neither established drug companies nor computer software manufacturers were pioneers in developing these technologies. On the whole, small firms did not invent the key genetic engineering techniques or Internet protocols. Rather, the enabling technologies were developed with government funds at academic institutions and research laboratories. It was the small entrants, however, who first seized upon the commercial opportunities. Even in areas where large firms have traditionally dominated, such as energy research, start-up firms appear to be playing an increasing role.

Not only do Schumpeter's arguments fail the test of experience, but systematic studies have generated little support for his belief in the innovative advantage of large firms. Over the years, economists have tried repeatedly to measure the relationship between firm size and innovation. While this literature is substantial, it is remarkably inconclusive. In part, its uncertain conclusions reflect the difficulty of doing such studies. Not only is it hard to measure innovative outputs and spending on research across a large number of firms, but often researchers struggle with what may be termed "selection biases." Consider, for instance, that it is very hard to get thorough information on firms that are not publicly traded. Thus, while we can see all of the large firms, which are almost invariably publicly held, we may only see the most successful small firms, since less stellar small firms are unlikely to complete a public offering.

While I will not inflict upon the reader a detailed review of the hundreds, if not thousands, of papers on this subject, it is worth highlighting that they give very little support to the claim that large firms are more innovative.[3] Much of this work has related measures of innovative discoveries—for example, R&D expenditures, patents, or inventions—to firm size. Initial studies were undertaken using the largest manufacturing firms; more recent works have employed larger samples and detailed data (e.g., studies employing data on firms' specific lines of business). Despite the improved methodology of recent studies, the results have remained inconclusive: the studies seem as likely to find a negative as a positive relationship, and even when a positive relationship between firms' size and innovation has been found, it has had little economic significance. For instance, one study concluded that a doubling of firm size increased the ratio of R&D to sales by only 0.2 percent.[4]

Whatever the relationship between a firm's size and its innovations, one of the relatively few things that researchers can agree on is the critical role played by new firms, or entrants, in many industries. The role of start-ups in emerging industries has been highlighted not just in many case studies, but also in systematic research. For instance, a study by Zoltan Acs and David Audretsch examined which firms developed some of the most important innovations of the twentieth century.[5] They documented the central contribution of new and small firms: these firms contributed almost half the innovations they examined. But they found that the contribution of small firms was not central in all industries. Rather, their role was a function of industry conditions: it was greatest in immature industries in which market power was relatively unconcentrated. These findings suggest that entrepreneurs and small firms play a key role in observing where new technologies can meet customers' needs, and rapidly introducing products.

What explains the apparent advantage of smaller firms? Much of it stems from the difficulty of large firms in fomenting innovation. For instance, one of Schumpeter's more perceptive contemporaries, John Jewkes, presciently argued:

> It is erroneous to suppose that those techniques of large-scale operation and administration which have produced such remarkable results in some branches of industrial manufacture can be applied with equal success to efforts to foster new ideas. The two kinds of organization are subject to quite different laws. In the one case the aim is to achieve smooth, routine, and faultless repetition, in the other to break through the bonds of routine and of ac-

cepted ideas. So that large research organizations can perhaps more easily become self-stultifying than any other type of large organization, since in a measure they are trying to organize what is least organizable.[6]

But this observation still begs a question: what explains the difficulties of larger firms in creating true innovations? Answers have been explored in recent work. In particular, there are at least three reasons why entrepreneurial ventures are more innovative:

- The first has to do with incentives. Normally, firms provide incentives to their employees in many roles, from salespeople to waiters. Yet large firms are notorious for offering employees little more than a gold watch for major discoveries. Why would the design of incentive systems for innovative tasks differ from that appropriate for humdrum tasks? The weak incentives in large firms may reflect the inherent riskiness and unpredictability of innovative projects, their length and complexity, and the number of parties who may make crucial contributions. Whatever the reason, there is a striking contrast between the very limited incentives at large corporate labs and the stock-option-heavy compensation packages at start-ups.

- Second, large firms may simply become ineffective at innovating. A whole series of authors have argued that incumbent firms frequently have blind spots, which stem from their single-minded focus on existing customers.[7] As a result, new entrants can identify and exploit market opportunities that the established leaders don't see.

- Finally, new firms may choose riskier projects. Economic theorists suggest that new firms are likely to pursue high-risk strategies, while established firms rationally choose more traditional approaches.[8] Hence, while small firms may fail more frequently, they are also likely to introduce more innovative products. This insight has been corroborated by, for instance, a study of the introduction of new software programs.[9] Its authors show that new firms are more effective at creating new software categories, while established firms have a comparative advantage in extending existing product lines.

One example of such innovation by a young firm that had a broad social impact was the African cell phone provider Celtel International.[10] The firm, begun in 1998, succeeded by taking advantage of the liberalizing African telecom industry of the 1990s and introducing services quickly absorbed by its customers. Because of the low average income, the African market had little penetration in either wireless or landline phones. Celtel grew by recognizing the large cash-based informal sector, addressing the low income of users by selling prepaid time in small, affordable units. In Tanzania, for instance, Celtel introduced per second instead of per minute calls that were the norm in the market and, by saving the consumer money, increased demand for its own services. Similarly, when Celtel obtained a permit for a microwave link between Congo-Kinshasa and Congo-Brazaville—capital cities on opposite sides of a river that were formerly linked by satellite—thus dropping the price of a call from one dollar per minute to twenty-eight cents, traffic increased by 700 percent.

While the growth process was not easy—the company was consistently short on cash and dependent largely on short-term loans from banks—its success was remarkable. By 2004, the company generated $147 million in earnings. The next year, the firm was acquired by Kuwait's Mobile Telecommunications Company in an all-cash transaction for $3.4 billion.

These initiatives had broad-reaching social consequences. In many cases, the cell phone has been as an income generator for village entrepreneurs. For instance, Celtel Tanzania sold personal call offices— briefcases with metered phones—to entrepreneurs who then sold the phone services on a per call basis. More generally, entrepreneurs on the continent have become more effective and profitable because of the spread of cell phones. Small-scale farmers and traders in particular have benefited from better knowledge of prices, allowing the market to converge to a point more beneficial to the small player. The cell phone is also used for low-cost banking targeting low-income users underserved by traditional banks. Celpay, Celtel's mobile commerce company, sees over 3 million transactions a month in the Democratic Republic of the Congo alone. The firm also has shown a preference for hiring locally at the community level for tasks like guarding generators or building towers, thus creating income for grassroots communities. Celtel and other cell phone service providers had a measurable effect on the national economies of the countries they entered. A 2007 report by the London Business School estimates that the average developing nation sees economic growth of 1.2 percent for every 10 percent increase in mobile users.[11]

The Special Case of Venture-Backed Firms

Recent studies have also highlighted the special advantage in innovation that belongs to certain entrepreneurs: those backed by venture capital firms. Considerable evidence shows that venture capitalists play an important role in encouraging innovation. The types of firms that they finance—whether young start-ups hungry for capital or growing firms that need to restructure—pose numerous risks and uncertainties that discourage other investors.

Where, then, does this advantage come from? The financing of young and restructuring firms is a risky business. Uncertainty and gaps in information often characterize these firms, particularly in high-technology industries. A lack of information makes it difficult to assess these firms, and permits opportunistic behavior by entrepreneurs after financing is received. To address these information problems, venture investors employ a variety of mechanisms that seem to be critical in boosting innovation.

The first of these devices is the screening process that venture capitalists use to select investment opportunities. This process is typically far more efficient than that used by other funders of innovation, such as corporate research and development laboratories and government grant-makers. For instance, most large, mature corporations tend to look at their existing lines of business when choosing projects to fund. Technologies outside the firm's core market, or projects that raise internal political tensions, often get shelved. In fact, many successful venture-backed start-ups are launched by employees who leave when their companies decline to pursue a promising technology.

Numerous studies have documented that typical venture capitalists use an exhaustive process to assess the large number of business plans they receive each year. One of the pioneering studies described a typical process:

> 1) Conversations with venture capitalists that ask[ed firm] to look at company; 2) Checked personal references of controller, vice-president, and president; 3) Met with company's founders and controller; 4) Conversation with loan officer at major insurance company. The insurance company's loan committee had turned down company's request for financing even though the loan officer recommended it; 5) Conversation with company's accountant . . .; 6) Conversation with local banker who slightly knew the company; 7) Conversation with banker who handles company's account; 8) Telephone conversation with director of company; 9) Talked to about 30 users; 10) Talked to two suppliers; 11) Talked to two competitors.[12]

One sophisticated individual investor, who follows an approach similar to venture firms, suggests it is likely to take up to 160 hours to properly screen an opportunity.[13] A leading venture capital group, Bessemer Venture Partners, prepared a "Due Diligence Booklet" for investors to complete for each potential investment. This fifty-page publication asked a large variety of questions about the industry, the company, the people, and the transaction itself.

How do venture capitalists make sense of all the data they gather during this assessment process? Certain measures are more important than others. After interviewing a large number of funds about their investment criteria, T. T. Tyebjee and A. V. Bruno described the most common criteria as follows:

1. Market Attractiveness (size, growth, and access to customers),

2. Product Differentiation (uniqueness, patents, technical edge, profit margin),

3. Managerial Capabilities (skills in marketing, management, finance and the references of the entrepreneur),

51

4. Environmental Threat Resistance (technology life cycle, barriers to competitive entry, insensitivity to business cycles and downside risk protection),

5. Cash-Out Potential (future opportunities to realize capital gains by merger, acquisition or public offering).[14]

Steve Kaplan and Per Strömberg, who examined the analyses that venture capitalists undertake when presenting potential transactions to their investment committees, identified a similar set of findings. They grouped the key decision-making criteria into three overall categories: (1) internal factors (quality of management, performance to date, funds at risk, influence of other investors, fit with the investment firm's existing portfolio, and monitoring costs and valuation); (2) external factors (market size and growth, competition and barriers to entry, likelihood of customer adoption, and financial market and exit conditions); and (3) difficulty of execution (nature of the product or technology, and the business strategy model).[15]

Another way in which venture capitalists screen transactions is through financial analysis. They carefully analyze the prospective returns from investments, conditional on the firm's success. They invest only if the expected return is suitably large. This requirement of a large return if the firm is successful stems from the high failure rates associated with venture capital investments. Only one-third of firms complete initial public offerings, typically the most attractive route through which to exit investments.[16] While some investments are exited successfully though acquisitions, in most cases they generate far lower returns. Despite all the care and expertise of venture capitalists, disappointment is the rule rather than the exception.

In addition to the careful interviews and financial analysis, venture capitalists usually make investments with other investors. One venture firm will originate the deal and look to bring in other venture capital firms. Involving other firms provides a second opinion on the opportunity. There is usually no clear-cut evidence that an investment will yield attractive returns. Having other investors approve the deal limits the likelihood of funding bad deals. This is particularly true when the company is early-stage or technology-based. Syndication also allows the venture capital firm to diversify. If venture capitalists had to invest alone in all the companies in their portfolio, they could make far fewer investments. By syndicating investments, the venture capitalist can invest in more projects and largely diversify away firm-specific risk.

The result of this detailed analysis is, of course, a lot of rejections: only about 0.5 to 1 percent of business plans are funded.[17] Inevitably, many good ideas are rejected as part of the assessment process. Most venture capitalists are embarrassed to admit these goofs, but Bessemer cheerily posts an "anti-portfolio" of great companies it passed over for various reasons.[18] And, of course, many companies are funded that ultimately prove to be disappointments.

When venture capitalists invest, they hold preferred stock rather than common stock. The significance of this distinction is that if the company is liquidated or otherwise returns money to the shareholders, preferred stock is paid before the common stock that entrepreneurs, as well as other, less privileged investors, hold. Moreover, venture capitalists add numerous restrictive covenants and provisions to the preferred stock. They may be able, for instance, to block future financings if they are dissatisfied with the valuation, to replace the entrepreneur, and to have a set number of representatives on (or even control of) the board of directors. In this way, if something unexpected happens (which is the rule rather than the exception with entrepreneurial firms), the venture investor can assert control. These terms vary with the financing round, with the most onerous terms reserved for the earliest financing rounds.

In addition to the initial selection process, the advice that venture firms provide to entrepreneurs and the postinvestment monitoring and control they exert support top-quality innovation. Venture capitalists also tend to spot more potential future applications of technology than larger, mature companies do, perhaps because older companies focus on narrower markets.

The staging of investments also improves the efficiency of venture capital funding. In large corporations, research and development budgets are typically set at the beginning of a project, with few interim reviews planned. Even if projects do get reviewed midstream, few of them are terminated when signs suggest they're not working out.

53

This contrasts with the venture capital process: once they make a decision to invest, venture capitalists frequently disburse funds in stages. The refinancing of these firms, termed "rounds" of financing, is conditional on achieving certain technical or market milestones. Proceeding in this fashion allows the venture capitalist to gather more information before providing additional funding, thus helping investors separate investments that are likely to be successful from those that are likely to fail. Managers of venture-backed firms have to return repeatedly to their financiers for additional capital, which allows venture capitalists to ensure that money is not squandered on unprofitable projects. Thus an innovative idea continues to be funded only if its promoters continue to execute, and as a corollary, projects that prove promising are able to access capital in a timely fashion.

Finally, venture capitalists provide intensive oversight of the firms they invest in. Michael Gorman and Bill Sahlman found that venture capitalists who responded to their survey spent about half their time monitoring an average of nine portfolio investments and serving on the boards for five of those nine companies.[19] They visited their companies relatively frequently, and spent an average of eighty hours a year on site with the company on whose board they served. Frequent telephone conversations amounted to another thirty hours per year for each company. In addition, they worked on the company's behalf by attracting new investors, evaluating strategy against new conditions, and interviewing and recruiting new management candidates.

Interviews with venture capitalists and entrepreneurs suggest that, as a consequence of these tools, venture capital plays an important role in boosting innovation. This assistance has two dimensions: accelerating growth and ensuring long-run success.

With support from venture capitalists, start-ups can invest in the research, market development, marketing, and strategizing they require to attain the scale necessary to go public. As a result, venture-backed firms tend to be considerably younger at the time that they go public, or first start trading in the market, than other companies. Table 3.1, which shows the age of U.S. venture-capital-backed and non-venture-capital-backed firms at the time they go public, captures this phenomenon.[20] The table shows the time in months from company founding

Table 3.1
Age of Firms (in Months) at the Time of Going Public

Months from Founding Date to IPO	Average		Median	
Venture Backed Firms	105		91	
Non-Venture Backed Firms	203		109	

Months from founding to IPO	Average		Median	
SIC Code	Venture-Backed	Non-Venture	Venture-Backed	Non-Venture
Pharmaceuticals - 2834	86	178	74	199
Semiconductors - 3674	120	175	103	95
Software - 7372	102	195	92	229
Business Services (mostly B2B) -7389	101	138	81	144

Note: Based on U.S. IPOs since 2003

to the issuing of equity in an initial public offering, both overall and in various industries. (We look at offerings between 2003 and September 2008, thus avoiding the atypical "bubble" years.) Overall, and across the industries, the venture-backed initial public offerings (IPOs) reached the public market sooner than the non-venture-backed group. Venture capitalists speed the development of companies because they help them pursue effective strategies while providing access to capital, if the companies are meeting their stated goals.

The evidence suggests that the early participation of venture firms — including their guidance, monitoring, shaping of management teams and boards, networking, and credibility — helps innovators sustain their success long after their company issues an IPO. By contrast, companies that go public without having had professional investors beforehand often encounter disappointment: they do not have the infrastructure in place, for example, financial reporting, investor communications, and strategic planning, to operate successfully as a public firm.

Two Illustrations

At this point, it's almost obligatory to illustrate the impact of venture capitalists with one of a few stories of real firms. Rather than discuss how Kleiner Perkins and Sequoia helped Google dominate the market for Internet searches, or how Accel and Greylock facilitated Facebook's climb into a dominant position in the crowded world of social networking, perhaps it would be more interesting to discuss some less well-known firms.

Consider, for example, the story of Lingtu.[21] This Beijing company makes digital maps for both individual and corporate applications. While we're all familiar with the power of mapping software both online and in mobile devices, these services are particularly important in China, where city streets are frequently a maze of winding, tiny lanes and where breakneck growth renders paper maps obsolete soon after they are printed.

By January 2003, Lingtu's founders—who had begun the firm four years previously—decided they needed help in thinking about strategic choices. Yes, the firm had built an impressive database of information about China's roadways, developed cutting-edge mapping software, and—important in a nation where maps are still regarded as sensitive information—obtained a license from the China State Bureau of Surveying and Mapping to create, digitize, and edit maps. But the plethora of new options left the founding team, which was dominated by engineers, struggling to decide which option to pursue. Observed Lingtu's CEO, Nengzhe Tang, "Sometimes I'm working so hard all I can see are . . . trees [and not the forest]. . . . Maps are like tofu, they can be prepared so many different ways."[22]

Shortly thereafter, Lingtu's team met Gobi Partners, a fund that from its inception in 2001 has focused single-mindedly on financing early-stage Chinese digital media companies. The three founders of Gobi had expertise in investment banking, the law, and software engineering, and had worked together at one of the pioneering Asian venture funds before launching their own firm. After an exhaustive due diligence process, Gobi invested a little over $2 million in Lingtu.

Gobi assisted the firm in a variety of ways in the next few years. First, it helped the firm prioritize the allocation of resources. As Tang commented, "Gobi gives us the forest view. . . . After we saw how they planned, we understood what it takes to move into big applications and how that could benefit us."[23] Second, Gobi introduced Lingtu to a number of corporations that were investors in Gobi's fund. These partners included IBM, which partnered with Lingtu to develop navigation and web map-search programs and supported the young firm in a winning bid to provide geographic information and software to telecommunications provider China Unicom, and NTT DoCoMo, which also served the lead investor in a subsequent financing round. Finally, the initial and subsequent financing rounds—including a $30 million round that also involved U.S.-based Oak Investment Partners and AllianceBernstein—allowed the firm to invest in technology and marketing to a much greater extent than previously.

The jury is still out on Lingtu, which remains privately held. It hopes to go public soon, though the battering that the Chinese stock market experienced in 2008 means that "soon" may take a while. But whatever its fate, venture capitalists played a critical role in transforming promising technology into a real business.

While venture capitalists often specialize in young technology companies, their reach can extend in other realms as well. To cite one example, Abraaj Capital, the leading private equity group in the Middle East, bought a one-third interest in April 2006 in National Air Services (NAS), a privately held aviation services and management company based in Riyadh, Saudi Arabia.[24]

To Abraaj, the deal was attractive for several reasons. The investment would allow the Dubai-based fund to gain access to the largest economy in the region and to a fast-growing sector that was typically closed to outside investors. But most importantly, Abraaj believed that the four-year-old firm's existing management was stumbling amid ambitious expansion plans, and that Abraaj could materially assist in the firm's growth.

After the deal closed, Abraaj assembled a team of fourteen specialists from its own ranks and outside the firm, who stayed for almost a year in Saudi Arabia. Shortly after its investment, the Abraaj team helped reorganize the company into three new business units, NAS Air, NetJets Middle East, and Al Khayala. Each of these units experienced substantial growth in the ensuing years, catalyzed in large part by Abraaj:

- In February 2007, the firm launched NAS Air, Saudi Arabia's first low-cost airline. Abraaj recruited a new CEO for NAS Air, Ed Winters, the former operating head at the British discount carrier easyJet. By the end of 2007, NAS Air had expanded to add more than 300 weekly flights and over twenty routes carrying nearly half a million passengers, making it Saudi Arabia's leading carrier in number of passengers. Orders were in place for more than forty planes.

- In 2007, private aviation service NetJets Middle East (which had held the franchise from Berkshire Hathaway's NetJets for Saudi Arabia) won the franchise rights to expand into new markets across the region.

- With Abraaj's help, the firm also launched Al Khayala, a luxury shuttle and charter service, in 2007.

Abraaj had planned to take the firm public to access further financing, but in June 2008 it sold its stake to a large Saudi investor. The implied valuation of the firm—more than twice that of Abraaj's initial investment—reflected in large part the value that had been created by the venture team, including the recruitment of new talent, the accomplishment of strategic initiatives, and the overcoming of regulatory and contractual hurdles.

Large-Sample Evidence

Clearly, venture capital exerts a major impact on the fate of individual companies. But does all this fund-raising and investing influence the overall economic landscape? How could such an influence be determined? And if it did exist, how would it be measured?

To assess this question, we can look at studies of the experience of the United States, the market with the most developed and seasoned venture capital industry. Although venture activity is particularly well developed in the United States, the reader might doubt whether this activity noticeably drives innovation: for most of past three decades, investments made by the entire venture capital sector totaled less than the research-and-development and capital-expenditure budgets of large, individual companies such as IBM, General Motors, or Merck. On the face of it, this suggests the business press has exaggerated the importance of the venture capital industry. High-tech start-ups make for interesting reporting, but do they really redefine the U.S. economy?

One way to explore this question is to examine the impact of venture investing on wealth, jobs, and other financial measures across several industries. Though it would be useful to track the fate of *every* venture-capital-financed company and find out where the innovation or technology ended up, in reality only those companies that have gone public can be tracked. Consistent information on venture-backed firms that were acquired or went out of business simply doesn't exist. Moreover, investments in companies that eventually go public yield much higher returns than support given to firms that get acquired or remain privately held.

These publicly traded firms have had an unmistakable effect on the U.S. economy. In September 2008, 895 firms were publicly traded on U.S. markets after receiving their private financing from venture capitalists (this figure does not include the firms that went public but were subsequently acquired or delisted). One way to assess the overall impact of the venture capital industry is to look at the economic "weight" of venture-backed companies in the context of the larger economy. Table 3.2, which documents the impact of venture capital in 2008, reveals some startling numbers.[25] By late 2008, venture-backed firms that had gone public made up over 13 percent of the total number of public firms in existence in the United States at that time. And of the total market value of public firms ($28 trillion), venture-backed companies came in at $2.4 trillion—8.4 percent.

Venture-funded firms also made up over 4 percent (nearly one trillion dollars) of total sales ($22 trillion) of all U.S. public firms at the time. And contrary to the general perception that venture-supported companies are not profitable, operating income margins for these companies hit an average of 6.8 percent—close to the average public-company profit margin of 7.1 percent. Finally, those public firms supported by venture funding employed 6 percent of the total public-

Table 3.2

Relative Status of Venture-Backed and Non-Venture Firms at the End of September 2008

	Number of Firms	Market Capitalization	Employees	Sales	Operating Income Before Depreciation	Net Income	Average Profit Margin
Venture-Backed	895	2,359,498	3,210	925,717	168,642	63,402	6.8%
Non-Venture	5,803	25,607,925	49,176	20,955,942	4,264,172	1,567,303	7.1%

Note: All dollar figures in millions; all employment figures in thousands.

company workforce—most of these jobs high-salaried, skilled positions in the technology sector. Clearly, venture investing fuels a substantial portion of the U.S. economy.

Venture investing not only supports a substantial fraction of the U.S. economy, it also strengthens particular industries. To be sure, it has relatively little impact on those dominated by mature companies— such as the manufacturing industries. That's because venture investors' mission is to capitalize on revolutionary changes in an industry, and the well-developed sectors often have a relatively low propensity for radical innovation.

But contrast mature industries with highly innovative ones, and the picture looks completely different. For example, companies in the computer software and hardware industry that received venture backing during their gestation as private firms represented more than 75 percent of the software industry's value. Venture-financed firms also play a central role in the biotechnology, computer services, and semiconductor industries. All of these industries have experienced tremendous innovation and upheaval in recent years. Venture capital has catalyzed change in these industries, providing the resources for entrepreneurs to generate substantial return from their ideas. In recent years, the scope of venture groups' activity has been expanding rapidly in the critical energy and environmental field, though the impact of these investments remains to be seen.

As these statistics suggest, venture capitalists create whole new industries and seed fledgling companies that later dominate them. The message is clear: the venture capital revolution drove the transformation of the U.S. economy in recent decades.

It might seem fairly easy to delineate the impact of venture capital on innovation. For instance, one could seek to explain across industries and time whether, controlling for R&D spending, venture capital funding has an impact on measures of innovation. But even a simple model of the relationship between venture capital, R&D, and innovation suggests that this approach is likely to give misleading estimates.

This is because both venture funding and innovation could be positively related to a third unobserved factor, the arrival of technological opportunities. Thus, there could be more innovation when there is more venture capital, not because the venture capital caused the innovation, but rather because venture capitalists reacted to a technological shock that was sure to lead to more innovation. To date, only a handful of studies have attempted to address this challenging interaction.

The first of these papers, by Thomas Hellmann and Manju Puri,[26] examines a sample of 170 recently formed firms in Silicon Valley, including both venture-backed and non-venture firms. Using questionnaire responses, they find evidence that venture capital financing is related to product market strategies and outcomes of start-ups. They find that firms that pursue an "innovator strategy" (a classification based on the content analysis of survey responses) are significantly more likely and faster to obtain venture capital. The presence of a venture capitalist is also associated with a significant reduction in the time taken to bring a product to market, especially for innovators (probably because these firms can focus more on innovating and less on raising money). Furthermore, firms are more likely to list obtaining venture capital as a significant milestone in the life cycle of the company than other financing events.

The results suggest significant interrelations between the type of investor and the product market, and a role of venture capital in encouraging innovative companies. But this does not definitively answer the question of whether venture capitalists cause innovation. For instance, we might observe personal injury lawyers at accident sites, handing out business cards in the hopes of drumming up clients. But just because the lawyer is at the scene of the car crash does not mean that he caused the crash. In a similar vein, the possibility remains that more innovative firms choose to finance themselves with venture capital, rather than venture capital causing firms to be more innovative.

In my work with Sam Kortum, I visited the same question.[27] Here we looked at the aggregate level: did the participation of venture capitalists in any given industry over the past few decades lead to more or less innovation? Does such an analysis escape the methodological problem illustrated by the personal injury lawyer at the accident scene, that is, mistaking effect for cause? To put the question another way, even if we see an increase in venture funding and a boost in innovation, how can we be sure that one caused the other?

We addressed these concerns about causality by looking back over the industry's history. In particular, a watershed in the history of venture capital was the U.S. Department of Labor's clarification of the Employee Retirement Income Security Act in the late 1970s, a change that freed pensions to invest in venture capital. This shift led to a sharp increase in the funds committed to venture capital. This type of external change should allow us to figure out what the impact of venture capital was, because it is unlikely to be related to how many or how few entrepreneurial opportunities there were to be funded.

Once these concerns with causality have been addressed, the results suggest that venture funding does have a strong positive impact on innovation. The estimated coefficients vary according to the techniques employed, but on average a dollar of venture capital appears to be *three to four* times more potent in stimulating patenting than a dollar of traditional corporate R&D. The estimates therefore suggest that venture capital, even though it on average amounted to less than 3 percent of corporate R&D in the United States from 1983 to 1992, was responsible for a much greater share—perhaps 10 percent—of U.S. industrial innovations in this decade.

A natural worry with this analysis is that it looks at the relationship between venture capital and patenting, not venture capital and innovation. It is possible that venture funding leads entrepreneurs to protect their intellectual property with patents rather than other mechanisms, such as trade secrets. Perhaps entrepreneurs can fool their venture investors by applying for a large number of patents, even if they protect modest advances. If this were true, the patents of venture-backed firms would likely be of lower quality than non-venture-backed patent filings.

How could this question of patent quality be investigated? One possibility is to check the number of patents that cite a particular patent.[28] Higher-quality patents, it has been shown, are cited by other innovators more often than lower-quality ones. Similarly, if venture-backed patents are lower quality, then companies receiving venture funding would be less likely to initiate patent-infringement litigation. (It makes no sense to pay money to engage in the costly process of patent litigation to defend low-quality patents.)

So what happens when patent quality is measured with these criteria? As it happens, the patents of venture-backed firms are more frequently cited by other patents and are more aggressively litigated—thus it can be concluded that they are of high quality. Furthermore, venture-backed firms more frequently litigate trade secrets, suggesting that they are not simply patenting frantically in lieu of relying on trade-secret protection. These findings reinforce the notion that venture-supported firms are simply more innovative than their non-venture-supported counterparts.

FINAL THOUGHTS

This chapter examines the first two pillars supporting the case for public intervention to promote venture activity. Both seem quite sturdy.

First, the link between innovation and growth is well established. More economic activity and a better quality of life depend vitally on a steady supply of new technologies and approaches. The need for innovation is widely accepted by governments around the world.

Second, there is a powerful link between innovation and new firms. Whether it is due to the stultifying bureaucracy that inhibits new ideas at large firms, the more powerful incentives new firms offer, or some other factor, entrepreneurs seem better at developing and commercializing new ideas. And no matter how one looks at the numbers, venture capital clearly serves as an important source industry for innovation, reflecting the fact that these investors both provide important guidance to young firms and relieve all-too-common capital constraints. This relationship is one that appears true across the world, though many of the systematic studies have focused on the well-developed American market.

All these arguments suggest that government interventions to boost entrepreneurial and venture capital activity may make sense. But it is not so simple, of course: for public intervention to boost venture capital and entrepreneurship, it has to be effective.

And this is by no means always the case. It is this complicated territory that we explore in the next chapter.

CHAPTER 4

THINGS GET MORE COMPLICATED

In the previous chapter, we highlighted the importance of innovation to economic growth, and the role that young firms, particularly those backed by venture investors, play in stimulating new ideas. When reviewing these propositions, we were able to point to a substantial body of academic research—and many less systematic (but perhaps more persuasive!) stories—suggesting that a strong relationship exists between new ventures and innovation.

But as we noted in the previous chapter's conclusion, these two facts alone are insufficient for us to come to a definitive conclusion. In particular, if government intervention in this arena is to make sense, it is necessary for the effort to be effective in stirring entrepreneurial and venture activity. And it is by no means certain that this is the case.

In this chapter, we'll review previous research and what it tells us about the effectiveness of government intervention. Here, alas, the evidence is less persuasive. On the one hand, there are many reasons why governments should be able to play a catalytic role. By its very nature, entrepreneurship is an activity that feeds on itself, which means that a public "jump start" may well be helpful. But on the other hand, government programs to boost venture activity have frequently fallen prey to incompetent decision-making or else to outright distortions by special interests. We'll discuss these challenging threats to effective government programs in this chapter.

WHY GOVERNMENTS CAN ENCOURAGE VENTURE ACTIVITY

Even if entrepreneurship and venture capital can play an important role in spurring innovation, it is natural to ask why *government* should intervene in these markets. Isn't this economic activity one that is best left to the private marketplace? Aside from the historical anecdotes alluded to in chapter 2, what case can be made for government intervention?

Beginning a Virtuous Cycle

The first rationale for government intervention lies in the fact that there is a "virtuous cycle" in entrepreneurship and venture capital. Activities by pioneering entrepreneurs and venture capitalists pave the way for subsequent generations: in a given city, it is far easier to recruit the staff for the one-hundredth start-up, or to find a lawyer to structure the one-hundredth financing, than the first.

Indeed, history is full of examples of pioneering firms that served as "entrepreneurship academies," from which other entrepreneurs sprung. The most famous example has already been briefly mentioned, Fairchild Semiconductor. The firm's origins had been Shockley Semiconductor Laboratory, which William Shockley founded in 1956.[1] After failing to lure his former colleagues from Bell Labs, he had hired some of the best graduates from U.S. engineering departments. But Shockley's autocratic style soon alienated many of the new hires. In 1957, eight key engineers—the Traitorous Eight, as they soon became known—left Shockley and formed their own company, Fairchild Semiconductor. While the company was successful in many respects, introducing the first commercially available integrated circuit and becoming one of the major players in Silicon Valley in the 1960s, it also saw frequent defections by engineers who founded their own firms. Among the semiconductor companies founded by its alumni were AMD (Advanced Micro Devices), Computer MicroTechnology, Cirrus Logic, Intel, LSI, and National Semiconductor—the key players in the industry in the decades to come. Other firms have played similar roles elsewhere, such as Minnesota-based device manufacturer Medtronic and the executive search firm Recruit in Japan.[2]

Several forms of information generation lead to this "virtuous cycle":

- Employees at large firms may initially be reluctant to "make the plunge" and join a start-up firm. Notions such as stock options

66

may seem alien and insufficient justification for the lower compensation and higher risk frequently associated with young firms. Over time, the great rewards that equity in young firms can bring, as well as the other benefits of working for a dynamic young firm, are increasingly appreciated.

- Much of the entrepreneurial process is an art rather than a science. The surest way to appreciate the issues at work in this setting, and to successfully navigate the many shoals that lurk to scuttle the unwary, is to live through a previous venture. With the proliferation of entrepreneurial ventures, there develops a cadre of seasoned, successful entrepreneurs, who are far more effective managers in these settings than their peers.

- Entrepreneurs become familiar with the trade-offs associated with venture capital financing. Initial disputes about the types of terms and conditions commonplace in venture financing are balanced with an appreciation for the types of gains possible with the involvement of a seasoned financier.

- Intermediaries such as lawyers and accountants become familiar with the venture process, and can better advise entrepreneurs and financiers alike.

- Institutional investors gain greater confidence that the sector in which venture capitalists are operating is a viable one, and become more willing to back funds.

- Venture capitalists more readily find peers with whom they can share transactions. The syndication of transactions is an important form of "judgment sharing," which allows a group of venture capitalists to make more effective decisions than if each one operated alone.[3]

An extensive body of economic thought in public finance discusses the circumstances in which it is appropriate for the government to offer subsidies. These works emphasize that subsidies are an appropriate response in the case of activities that generate positive "externalities," or benefits to others that are not captured by the firm or individual undertaking the activity. Thus, governments often provide subsidies to firms that invest in pollution control equipment or individuals who install solar power. Most of the benefits from their investment to reduce pollution and greenhouse gasses will benefit all of us, not the firm itself. To encourage investments that primarily benefit other firms and all of society, public subsidies are often an appropriate response.

In a similar manner, pioneering entrepreneurs and venture capitalists generate positive externalities that benefit others. It is precisely when such externalities are present that public interventions–whether tax incentives, regulatory shifts, or more direct measures—are justified. These spillovers to other firms are likely to be particularly important in the youngest days of the entrepreneurial sector or the venture capital industry, when pioneering new ventures and investment groups are just getting established. These relationships suggest that government may have an important role in priming the pump for additional entrepreneurial and venture activity during the industry's inception. Once the industry reaches a critical mass, a process that will take years or even decades, the case for public intervention will wane.

This claim can be supported by the low returns that many pioneering venture funds have garnered. For instance, venture and growth equity funds active in the developing world—which I define here as countries other than Canada, the United States, western Europe, Australia, Japan, and New Zealand—have garnered very disappointing returns over the past two decades. If one takes the simple average of the rates of returns of these funds, they have generated an annual return of 3.8 percent. The weighted average (that is, when we count larger funds more) is even grimmer: −1.5 percent.[4] These returns are less than those that would have come from holding the safest Treasury bills, much less public stocks.

A natural interpretation of these patterns is that they reflect the difficulties of undertaking successful investments in markets such as China and Russia, where regulatory uncertainties, inexperienced entrepreneurs, and a problematic judiciary make investment challenging. But it appears that if one looked at the returns from the early days of the U.S. venture industry, one would see a similar picture. For instance, the pioneering venture American Research and Development, whose history we discussed in chapter 2, had an annual return of only 14.7 percent despite its "home run" return from Digital Equipment.[5] There were many dozens of funds during the decades in which ARD was active, most of which are forgotten. Given that the funds that have faded in the mists of time were in all probability far less successful than ARD, the returns of the U.S. venture industry during its early years are likely to have been no better than the emerging market funds in their initial years. This pattern suggests that no matter how promising the returns of entrepreneurial activity ultimately are, in a venture market's early years, low returns are likely.

Providing Certification

A second rationale for government involvement lies in its ability to provide a stamp of approval. A growing body of empirical research suggests that new firms, especially technology-intensive ones, may receive insufficient capital to fund all value-creating projects. Why cannot entrepreneurs get funded? A frequent source of blame is information asymmetries. The entrepreneur invariably knows more about the central technology than anyone else. But outside investors cannot uncritically accept the claims that entrepreneurs make, since they have so much to gain from getting funding (and are likely to be excessively optimistic in any case). As a result, great ideas may go unfunded.

Indeed, economists have studied the impact of capital constraints—the inability of firms to raise enough money, typically because potential investors lack sufficient information—and documented the breadth of this problem. An inability to obtain external financing limits many forms of business investment.[6] Investments in research and development are no exception: capital constraints also appear to limit expenditures, at least in smaller firms.

As we discussed in the last chapter, venture capitalists specialize in financing this type of firm. They address their need for information through a variety of mechanisms. Other investors, aware that venture capitalists are astute investors in these settings, should be able to follow their lead, and back companies that they finance: the certification

69

that venture investments provide should unlock the door to much more funding. Thus, expenditures by the government to catalyze venture funds could have an "add-on" effect. Other investors, confident that information deficits had been overcome, could confidently follow the venture investors' lead.

Taking this argument even further, government investments may also have a certifying effect. Why not just rely on the venture capital industry to provide a stamp of approval? A primary reason is that venture capitalists back only a tiny fraction of the technology-oriented businesses begun each year. In 2000, a record year for venture disbursements, just over 2,200 U.S. companies received venture financing for the first time; in 2007, the number was 1,279.[7] Yet the Small Business Administration estimates that, in recent years, about one million new businesses have started up annually.[8] Furthermore, private venture funds have concentrated on a few industries: for instance, in 2000, fully 46 percent of the funding went to Internet-related companies. More generally, 92 percent of the funding went to firms specializing in information technology or health care. By 2008, the spotlight had shifted to renewable energy, among other topics: almost 16 percent of the funds in the second quarter of 2008 went to companies in the "energy and industry" category. Whatever the flavor of the moment, many promising firms in other industries are *not* attracting venture capitalists' notice, perhaps reflecting "herding" by venture capitalists into particular areas, a problem that finance theory suggests affects institutional investors.[9] If government programs can identify and support these neglected firms, they might provide the stamp of approval these high-potential, underfunded firms need to succeed.

But if government officials are going to address such problems as herding, they will need to overcome the many information asymmetries and identify the most promising firms or else choose venture groups that can. Otherwise, their efforts are likely to be counterproductive.[10] Is it reasonable to assume that government officials can overcome problems that private sector financiers cannot? This possibility is not implausible. For instance, specialists at agencies that concentrate on funding health care and defense research may have considerable insight into which biotechnology or advanced materials companies are the most promising from a scientific perspective (though of course, interesting science and engineering does not always translate into a profitable company), while the traditional financial statement analysis undertaken by bankers would be of little value. In general, the certification hypothesis suggests that these signals provided by government awards are likely to be particularly valuable in technology-intensive industries where traditional financial measures fall short.

Creating Knowledge Flows

A third rationale for public entrepreneurship and venturing initiatives is that knowledge spillovers may result.

An extensive literature has documented that innovation is one area where spillovers are commonplace.[11] These spillovers take several forms:

- For instance, a firm may make a substantial investment in a new product only to see a rival capture most of the sales and profits: think about SaeHan Information Systems, which introduced the first portable digital music player in 1998. While the Korean manufacturer solved the key technical problems associated with the device, its ultimate sales were a tiny fraction of Apple's iPod.

- In other cases, another firm that develops a related product may get most of the profits. For instance, the bulk of the rewards associated with personal computers since their inception in the early 1980s have not gone to manufacturers such as Hewlett Packard and Lenovo, or to application developers such as Lotus or WordPerfect, but rather to two firms that contribute other essential inputs into these computers, the microprocessors (Intel) and the operating system (Microsoft).

- Finally, innovations may end up not being very profitable, while very beneficial to society as a whole. One example may be Amazon, which after a decade of operation has not come close to earning back the capital provided by its investors. At the same time, the firm has made books and other merchandise much more available to many who do not live near major bookstores or specialty retailers.

71

Thus, in many instances, the firms pursuing an innovation get fewer benefits than society as a whole. As a result, left to their own devices, companies will do less research than desirable. But with government subsidies, firms may be encouraged to invest the socially ideal amount of funds in R&D.

One way that economists try to get a handle on the extent of under-funding of research is to compare the return that a company gets from undertaking research and that which society as a whole earns. Such an exercise is easier said than done: measuring the social rate of return is very tricky, and requires quite a few assumptions along the way. After reviewing a wide variety of studies using quite different methodologies, Zvi Griliches estimates that the gap between the private and social rate of return is substantial, probably equal to between 50 percent and 100 percent of the private rate of return.[12] Thus, if a firm earned a 10 per-cent rate of return on its own investment in research, society would be earning 15 to 20 percent.

While few studies have examined how these gaps vary with firms' characteristics, a number of case-based analyses suggest that the differ-ences between social and private returns are especially large among small firms.[13] These organizations may be particularly unlikely to ef-fectively defend their intellectual property positions or to extract most of the profits from their discoveries when competing against larger firms. As a result, it may make sense for governments to fund young research-intensive firms, even if the direct financial returns from these investments are somewhat less than would be reasonable given the risks that are taken on.

Taken together, these arguments suggest that subsidies to entrepre-neurs and venture firms can have multiple benefits. But, as we will soon see, the logic is not so straightforward.

THE CASE AGAINST GOVERNMENT INTERVENTION

The arguments outlined above implicitly assume that, once a problem needing public intervention is identified, the government can dispas-sionately address it. But this is a substantial leap. Government officials with the best of intentions can take counterproductive steps, and in some cases, their intentions are not the best. Distortions may result from government subsidies, as interest groups or politicians direct subsidies to benefit themselves. In this section, we'll explore how intervention can go very wrong.

Incompetence

These basic insights have been developed in an extensive literature on political economy and public finance. The first concern has to do with the competence of government. In many instance, officials may be manifestly inadequate to the task of managing entrepreneurial or innovative firms.

Much of the literature has addressed the quality of governmental efforts in general, rather than focusing on programs to enhance venture activity. Nonetheless, it suggests several clues to where the ability successfully to design and implement investment initiatives is likely to be found:

- Nobel laureate Douglass North has argued that as nations become wealthier, their ability to invest in government institutions grows.[14] Moreover, citizens and businesses are likely to demand better governmental services. As a result, nations with more wealth per citizen should have better governments. (Of course, the relationship could actually go the other way: countries could *become* rich because they have better governments.)

- Several political scientists and political economists have argued that ethnic homogeneity in societies is associated with better governments.[15] In diverse societies, the political winners all too often have focused their energies on expropriating wealth (or worse) from the other ethnic groups and enact measures that reinforce their hold on power. These steps are unlikely to lead to good government, to say the least!

- A growing "law and finance" literature suggests that there is a considerable amount of historical accident, or what economists sometimes call "path dependency," in how governments work.[16] For instance, many nations today adhere to either the common law or civil law tradition, legal systems that originally developed in England on the one hand and France and Germany on the other, and then spread through the world via colonization, conquest, or voluntary imitation. These traditions appear to have powerful impacts on how governments work, though it is not immediately obvious how these differing legal systems play out.

A 1998 paper by four leading economists in the "law and finance" literature tries to assess the extent to which these three considerations shape broad measures of governmental performance.[17] The results indicate a positive correlation between per capita income and government performance: rich nations, not surprisingly, have better governments than poor ones. In addition, more homogeneous countries, measured using languages spoken and ethnicity, have better governments than more diverse ones. In addition, government origin seems to matter: common-law countries, such as Great Britain and the United States, have better governments than civil law (particularly, the French civil law) or socialist law-based countries, highlighting the importance and influence of historical circumstances.

A flagrant example of government incompetence in promoting innovative activities comes indeed from France. The French government's efforts to encourage high-technology entrepreneurship over the past few decades have seen, to put it kindly, a series of miscues.

Consider, for instance, efforts to promote the electronics industry in the 1980s.[18] Following the ascension of François Mitterrand and the Socialist Party in 1981, the government spent about $6 billion to acquire a number of lumbering electronics giants, including CII Honeywell Bull and Thomson. Meanwhile, a number of promising smaller firms in the industries were either acquired directly by the government or pressured into merging with the giants.

The results were an unmitigated disaster. At the existing firms, once the government subsidies were in place, a tide of red ink turned into a torrent, with annual subsidies for annual losses growing from $226 million in 1980 to $4.6 billion in 1982. The vast majority of the ideas championed by young firms were extinguished as they became part of stultifying bureaucracies. Nor did the government put any real pressure on the established firms to develop their younger partners' ideas: the public bureaucrats' single-minded focus was on preserving employment at large existing factories. The contrast with Taiwan's successful efforts to stimulate its computer industry in the 1990s, where numerous subsidies were given to small firms with the expectation that many would fail but a few succeed brilliantly, could not be more stark.[19]

Even if we look just at the primary goal of the French government, their efforts to preserve jobs at existing French computing employers were essentially futile. The government was forced to sell off many firms, with attendant job losses, in the face of a political uproar over the size of the subsidies. Even companies that it continued to hold, such as Bull (in which the government held a majority stake until 1997), employment fell to 8,000 from a peak of 44,000 in 1991.

Nor are such ill-conceived interventions confined to the distant decades in France. Consider the efforts to create a high-technology cluster in Brittany.[20] The motivations that drove this effort were reasonable. Brittany had long been a hub for naval shipbuilding, indeed since the seventeenth century. As the French government cut back sharply on military procurement in the mid-1990s (domestic defense acquisition spending fell by nearly 40 percent between 1993 and 1997, even before adjusting for inflation), the dislocation that cutbacks would cause was a natural political issue.

But the solution—to create a French Silicon Valley in Brittany, with a focus on electronics—was remarkably ill-considered. Not only was there a limited entrepreneurial tradition in this region, but the shipyard was a significant share of all industrial activity. Recall that we saw in chapter 2 that both the region's entrepreneurial tradition and industrial backbone were important in the creation of Silicon Valley. But rather than a nascent hub of high-productivity innovation, Brittany was—and remains—dominated by lower-productivity industries.[21] This development route appears to have been decided upon in Paris, with little consultation with either local political leaders or potential entrepreneurs or business leaders. Moreover, after announcing an ambitious initiative for Brittany, funding was trimmed as more and more regions were highlighted for incentives.

One illustration of the government's strategy was the investment in broadband networks across the province. The provincial and national governments spent significant resources to build a network, in the hopes of stimulating research-intensive businesses in Brittany. Large subsidies were paid to French Telecom to develop the network, and the costs of users were subsidized. The assumption behind this expenditure was that the new infrastructure would stimulate entrepreneurial technology-oriented businesses that would be formed to take advantage of the network.

While some government-funded research centers did benefit from the spending, the anticipated benefits to entrepreneurship were not realized. As the OECD's (Organisation for Economic Cooperation and Development) assessment concluded, "It has not yet really taken off on the business side. The indirect benefits from the promotion of broadband have not really become apparent."[22] Instead, most of the benefits from the subsidies were captured by French Telecom and publicly funded universities. More generally, while the subsidies and science parks did attract multinationals and French firms to locate there, the impact of the initiative was blunted by the difficulties in telecommunications in the early 2000s and that of the Paris-based giant, Alcatel-Lucent, more specifically.

But the French misadventures, though notable for the size of expenditures, do not plumb the depths of governmental incompetence. There are so many examples that it is hard to know where to begin. Consider, for instance, the Tenant Opportunities Program (TOP), launched by U.S. Department of Housing and Urban Development in 1988 to promote entrepreneurship. It was rolled out at 816 public housing projects between 1988 and 1997.[23] The program was not intended to promote high-technology development, but rather more modest enterprises such as handmade toy manufacturing and childcare operations.

The program in the District of Columbia was emblematic of the problems TOP encountered. It provided $2.8 million to help thirty-one complexes in the area, which were chosen through a competitive process. But while the use of the funds was supposed to be monitored by the HUD's Washington field office, it did not have enough staff for the task. Instead, the District Housing Authority hired consultants to oversee the spending (a number of whom turned out to be related to or friends of Authority officials and members of its board of directors). Many of these consultants did not supervise the projects. In fact, a subsequent audit discovered that the majority of funds ended up in the pockets of the board members and the consultants themselves. Even as the incompetence of the consultants was revealed in the initial projects, the Authority continued to approve their use at other housing complexes.

Moreover, with no supervision and little guidance, the residents of the housing projects did not wisely spend the funds that reached them. The local councils funded efforts like Circuit City shopping expeditions and "training" trips to Las Vegas. A comment by one observer was that "word got around there was money . . . they knew they didn't have to do anything for it."[24]

Many other parts of the United States would give the District of Columbia some competition for the hall of ignominy. Kansas would definitely be a leading candidate.[25] In 1970s and 1980s, the state legislature sought to boost economic development in the state. Rather than appropriating funds for this purpose, which would have meant higher taxes and angry voters, the legislature simply mandated that the Kansas Public Employees Retirement System (KPERS), the pension for the state's employees, loan money to local businesses, and similarly to Kansas real estate developers. (The legislators somehow forgot to ask the public retirees if this is how they wanted their savings invested.) By the mid-1980s, a full 20 percent of the multi-billion-dollar pension had been earmarked for these homegrown investments.

Rather than undertaking the investments themselves, the state recruited two local investment firms to handle Kansas Investment Fund, as it was called. By the mid-1980s, frustrated at the slow investment pace, the state changed its instructions to the investment groups. Instead of backing firms that were "relatively substantial, seasoned and in sound financial condition," they were now ordered to include new or expanding Kansas businesses that were unable to get credit elsewhere. The change of policy undoubtedly had an effect: the investment firms, which collected a fee on each transaction and had little supervision from KPERS, began putting money to work much more quickly. And they made some high-risk choices indeed. $14 million went to a manufacturer of microcomputer memories that never saw a profit, $8 million into a steel fabricating plant that soon went belly-up, and $6.5 million to a start-up that was going to develop a revolutionary hydrogen-based energy source, and so forth. The most memorable investment was doubtless $65 million in loans to a local savings-and-loan that soon thereafter was seized by regulators as insolvent. Its loan portfolio, subsequent investigations revealed, included an uncompleted Hungarian film about a man-eating bear chasing a rock-and-roll band—and a $40 million loan to the KPERS's chairman. In all, the Kansas Investment Fund lost the state's pensioners and taxpayers $265 million, or about 7 percent of the pension's assets at the time. After thirteen years of litigation and $28 million in legal fees, the state recovered $41 million of those losses. (The chairman ended up being ordered to perform 200 hours of community service.)

These examples all involve government leaders who did not think carefully about realistic market opportunities and how subsidies would affect behavior. But a failure to understand the basic nature of the entrepreneurial process is also a frequent problem. One of the crucial patterns among high-growth ventures is that, at best, there are only a few very large winners. The typical outcome is disappointing. In the language of statistics, the distribution is a very skewed one. While getting comprehensive data on the returns of individual start-ups is almost impossible, we can look at the distribution of success of the venture funds that back them. Even though each fund typically invests in multiple deals, the bulk of the returns come from a few funds. Nor is the pattern unique to the United States. (Figure 4.1 shows distributions of returns of U.S. venture funds; figure 4.2 depicts the same pattern for European funds.)[26]

Yet in many cases, government officials proceed under the assumption that success is the typical outcome. One illustration of this unwarranted optimism is the disastrous history of most loan programs to finance high-growth entrepreneurial businesses.[27] In many cases, governments have launched these efforts under the assumption of high repayment rates. But these programs have a fundamental issue:

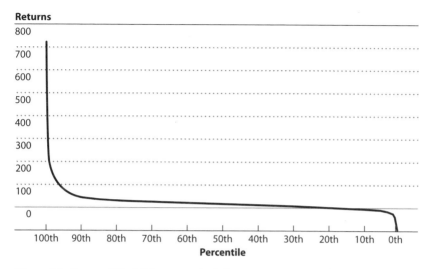

Figure 4.1. Returns (%) of U.S. venture funds from inception to March 31, 2008

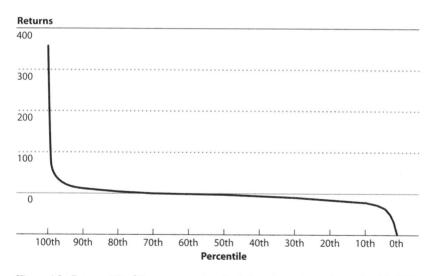

Figure 4.2. Returns (%) of European venture funds from inception to December 31, 2007

they do not share potential upside returns, but assume a significant portion of downside risks. For example, the Business Development Fund was established in Denmark to provide high-risk loans to high-technology projects in start-ups and established enterprises. Generous provisions for renegotiation were put in place, so entrepreneurs whose project proved disappointing were not pressured to return the money. As a result, the Fund (prior to a 2001 major reform) shared the downside risk with entrepreneurs, but received only a modest fixed interest for commercially successful projects. More than 60 percent of total funding was lost on the 900 initial projects the Fund supported.

Similarly, loan guarantee programs—which transfer to the public sector part of the risk of loans to innovative firms—have a mixed track record. Again, success hinges on a program's ability to achieve a low default rate while providing loans to borrowers that would otherwise not have been funded. Examples of loan guarantee programs include Canada's Small Business Loans Act program, the French OSEO-Garantie initiative, and the United Kingdom's Small Firms Loan Guarantee Scheme. The assumption that defaults will be low is frequently too optimistic: most guarantee schemes have not been sustainable without substantial subsidies. Moreover, letting a third party do the lending—most often a bank—often leads to "moral hazard" problems: the bank may be far more casual about evaluating the potential borrower when ultimately the bank's money is not at risk. For instance, a study of the French scheme finds that the probability that a small business borrower goes bankrupt in the four years after taking out a loan goes from 9 percent if the loan does not have a government guarantee up to a stratospheric 21 percent if it does (even after controlling for the differing risk profile of the guaranteed borrowers).[28] Thus, a lack of foresight about the incentives government programs set up can be very costly indeed.

Capture

These tales of public incompetence seem bad enough. But much of economists' attention has been focused on a darker problem that affects these and similar programs. Rather than worrying about government incompetence, many researchers have focused on the theory of "regulatory capture." This hypothesis suggests that entities, whether part of government or industry, will organize to capture the direct and indirect subsidies that the public sector hands out.[29]

This sounds terribly abstract, but it has very real consequences. A few examples from my home state, the Commonwealth of Massachusetts, illustrate the phenomenon of capture and how costly it can be:

- In some cases, groups organize to capture subsidies being handed out by government officials. For instance, when Massachusetts governor Deval Patrick sought a billion-dollar initiative to promote biotechnology research, legislators—working in concert with local university officials—sought to ensure that funds would go to their own districts.[30] To cite just the most egregious example, $49.5 million was allocated to a science center at the Massachusetts College of Liberal Arts in North Adams even though the college does not have a graduate program in science. Three local three university presidents—Drew Faust of Harvard, Susan Hockfield of MIT, and Jack Wilson of the University of Massachusetts—who might be expected to be enthusiastic about public funding for research, instead criticized the bill's emphasis on individual earmarks.

- In other occasions, regulators create opportunities for groups to garner substantial indirect gains. For instance, Massachusetts is unique among the fifty states in requiring that a local or state policeman must be present at all road construction projects.[31] (Everywhere else in the country, a flagman—earning only a small fraction of what the policeman does—is sufficient.) Of course, the argument is made by the police unions that this enhances public safety, but for some reason the statistical evidence does not support the claim that the presence of a policeman sitting in his patrol car munching donuts reduces accident rates!

- Nor are these captures confined to public sector entities or employees. A law passed three-quarters of a century ago effectively limits the sale of beer and wine to liquor stores and grocery stores with fewer than four licenses statewide. Why this distinction? Once again, a powerful lobby of beer distributors and small liquor stores has blocked alterations to this policy, which allows them to charge inflated prices without competition from major supermarket chains.

Economists point out that these capture problems are not seen everywhere evenly. Rather, they tend to appear where there are individuals or firms who stand to gain substantial benefits and whose collective political activity is not too difficult to arrange. The police unions are highly vocal and march to the State House whenever the ending of police details is proposed. Meanwhile, those bearing the costs of the extra $100 million or so that ends up in police officers' pockets each year—whether borne by a store owner seeking to widen a driveway or a homeowner paying property tax—find it much harder to undertake concerted action.

But certainly the capture of handouts is not a game that only large entities play. As Nobel laureate George Stigler points out, even very small firms can organize to benefit from public largess. For instance, industries like trucking and beauty salons have been traditionally covered by exhaustive regulations, which have made it difficult for new parties to enter the market. The lack of new competition has meant higher prices than would be the case otherwise. Despite the fact that these industries have traditionally been dominated by smaller operators, they have succeeded in getting the public sector to indirectly subsidize their profits.

If we turn to public efforts to boost entrepreneurial firms, capture problems can manifest themselves in several ways. Firms may seek transfer payments that directly increase their profits, and politicians may acquiesce to transfers to politically connected companies.

In fact some scholars have gone so far as to argue that there are two classes of entrepreneurs, some who create value, and others who simply extract profits from the system. Two closely related papers[32] regale readers with stories and analyses about various characters in history— whether Chinese mandarins, medieval nobles and monks, and lawyers through time and in all continents—who were very energetic in pursuing wealth for themselves while adding little to society as a whole. Whatever we may feel personally about monks or lawyers, the papers plausibly argue that encouraging the assemblage of wealth without attention to the broader impacts on society is a recipe for disaster. (Whether we believe the statistical analysis in one of the papers, which classifies countries as those with "good" and "bad" entrepreneurship on the basis of the number of graduates with engineering and legal degrees, is another story!)

We have already seen instances of capture in the tales related above: for instance, the way in which established players like France Telecom and local universities obtained much of the funding intended to boost entrepreneurial activity in Brittany. This phenomenon is also seen in large-sample studies.

Consider, for instance, two evaluations of programs to help firms to conduct research spending. These studies were done in very different markets, high-tech Israel and Spain, which remains dominated by traditional manufacturing firms.[33] The details of the programs differed as well.

Yet despite the different economies and programs, the analyses painted a very similar picture. These subsides appear to boost research spending among small firms, in particular leading a number of modest entities to start R&D programs that would have not done so otherwise. Presumably, these firms found it hard to raise capital by other means, such as from venture capitalists or banks, and these subsidies allowed them to undertake promising projects. Among larger firms, the impact was much weaker: the public funds seem to stimulate less research, and in the Israeli case, established firms may have even cut back their own research in response to public grants.

And yet in both cases, most of the actual subsidies went to larger firms that would have performed innovative activities even had they not received the subsidy. Presumably these larger concerns, being more adept at playing the game of winning government awards, managed to commandeer the funds, even though they were much less likely to fulfill the program's goals. The goals of the programs' designers were thus subverted.

The phenomenon of capture also has an even darker side. In other instances, it is the organizations that are mandated to help entrepreneurs—the very ones who proclaim they are helping smaller ventures—who manage to capture much of the returns for themselves.

Consider the Australian Building on Information Technology Strengths (BITS) program.[34] This effort was launched in 1999, with $158 million to "promote innovation and commercial success in the information industries by encouraging the creation and growth of new high technology firms."[35] BITS was catalyzed by the influx of funds that Australian government obtained when it sold its 17 percent interest in the telecommunications company Telstra. The centerpiece of the program, accounting for half of the initial spending, was the creation of eleven incubator centers for small and medium-sized firms in the information technology and telecommunication sector.

The government argued that given information gaps (discussed in chapter 3), which made it difficult for them to attract investment, young Australian technology firms were not receiving enough funding. By providing financing and advice, the incubators could increase the number of small entities in the information technology business and the success of the start-up firms. In 2001, as part of a package of innovation legislation, BITS was awarded further funding. Again, in 2004, at the end of the original five-year span of the program, BITS received an extra $36 million in funding, extending the program to 2008.

These renewals might suggest that the program was an unqualified success. But two evaluations completed before the additional funding was allocated paint a somewhat different picture. In particular, they suggest that while the program had been very successful for the incubators and individuals running these incubators, for many of the entrepreneurs, the picture was not so clear.

In particular, the proportion of funds accruing to the incubators, as opposed to the firms that the legislation was ultimately trying to help, attracted criticism. At the typical incubator, most of funding went to the incubator managers themselves, in order to compensate them for management advice and other services to the entrepreneurial firms: seven of the incubators gave less than 50 percent of funding in cash to the incubated firms. One example was the incubator operated by Allen and Buckeridge Seed Stages Ventures, where ultimately a mere 31 percent of the BITS funding went to the start-ups. By way of contrast, the incubator that had the most successful entrepreneurial firms, InQbator, provided 95 percent of the funding to the companies in its portfolio.

Not only were the bulk of the funds going to the incubator managers, but in a number of cases they were actually hindering the progress of the firms. Start-ups were actually limited in their ability to shop for the best service providers: instead of finding a specialist lawyer to negotiate a licensing deal, for instance, they were forced by the incubators to use the in-house counsel (for whose services the incubator managers charged a substantial markup). The quality of the advice often did not compare with that offered by more experienced lawyers and accountants in private practice. Adding insult to injury, many of the fees charged by the incubator managers, such as for rent and telephone, were considerably above market levels. But facing the possibility of expulsion if they did not use the incubators' services, many of the firms believed they had no choice but to agree. Unsurprisingly, more successful incubators like InQbator and BlueFire were more willing than the others to allow incubatees to obtain professional services from elsewhere.

To the government's credit, when the BITS incubator program was provided with an extra $36 million in funding in 2004, strings were attached. The continuation of the program had stricter terms, with further funding to be allocated only to incubators that were already funded under the program and were high performing.[36]

This phenomenon of capture is by no means unique to Australia. We've already alluded to venture promotion programs, such as the SBIC program in the United States, that continue to exist long after they've exhausted their usefulness. The presence of a vocal "subsidy lobby"—typically, trade associations representing groups that are benefiting far more from the subsidies than the entrepreneurs the programs are designed to help—is typically the root cause.

Final Thoughts

The final pillar on which the case for public intervention in venture activity rests is the claim that public intervention can be effective. Unfortunately, this argument is undoubtedly the wobbliest.

Certainly, entrepreneurial and venture capital activity exhibits many of the same features as other activities that receive public subsidies:

- It is much easier being an entrepreneur when one has many peers, which makes the task of initial pioneers particularly hard.

- The government can presumably provide certification to little-known entities.

- The knowledge generated by any one venture is likely to benefit many others.

But the same pathologies that bedevil many government efforts to provide subsidies are likely to emerge when the target is entrepreneurship. Entrepreneurial activities are by their nature highly uncertain and unpredictable, which means errors are common. And this uncertain environment means that those who want to direct subsidies to themselves may be able to operate with little scrutiny.

In the next four chapters, we'll turn from the "thirty-thousand-foot level" where we have been dwelling to a much closer look at the design and implementation of investment programs. The chapters will seek to understand what common mistakes governments make when putting these programs into practice, and how they can be avoided.

PART TWO

THREADING THE NEEDLE

CHAPTER 5

THE NEGLECTED ART OF SETTING THE TABLE

In recent years, many nations in Europe, Asia, and the Americas, as well as local and regional governments, have adopted initiatives to stimulate new ventures. While these programs' precise structures have differed, the efforts have been predicated on the rationales delineated in the preceding chapters. While some of the programs have been dramatic successes, governments worldwide have also squandered many billions of dollars on ill-conceived efforts. In some cases, these programs have even left their entrepreneurial sectors in worse shape than before. In the next four chapters, we'll seek to understand what works and what doesn't.

Government initiatives to simulate new venture activity can be divided into three broad categories. The first two focus on creating a more hospitable environment in which entrepreneurs and venture capitalists can operate; the final one encompasses direct interventions to boost the availability of financing. In economic terms, the initial interventions can be seen as boosting the demand for venture capital; and the final one as increasing the supply.

Looking across many nations and decades, we can see clearly that the third set of programs have had a magnetic appeal for politicians and bureaucrats alike. Maybe it is simply a lot more fun handing money out to entrepreneurs than worrying about whether legal rules are conducive to efficient contracting. Or perhaps boosting funding lends itself to the kind of monkey business described in the section titled "Capture" in chapter 4. But whatever the reason, the process of table-setting—of ensuring that the environment is favorable to entrepreneurs and venture investors alike—has been far too neglected. In this chapter, we'll look at ways that governments can freshen the environment for entrepreneurs.

ENHANCING THE ENTREPRENEURIAL CLIMATE

The first set of initiatives we'll look at has sought to boost the attractiveness of the climate for entrepreneurship. No matter how many inducements are offered to make venture investments, without attractive investment opportunities the venture industry is unlikely to be sustainable.

The most dramatic example of a country that has understood this lesson is Singapore. Singapore has developed a dazzling array of policies designed to promote entrepreneurial activity. Many of them, to be sure, involve direct subsidies to entrepreneurs and venture funds.

But the government, after trying various direct subsidy efforts in the 1990s, soon realized that more was required.[1] For instance, while numerous venture firms had been formed in response to government incentives, most tended to focus on investing in mature companies that were already profitable rather than in raw start-ups. On a more fundamental level, government leaders feared that the consequence of a conservative social environment and the extensive government intervention in the economy would be an unwillingness to take risks. Moreover, the abundant supply of attractive engineering positions for graduates of top schools led to their unwillingness to explore entrepreneurial options. Worried about the implications of these patterns for Singapore's long-term competition with China and other burgeoning economies, the government launched a variety of "indirect" initiatives, focusing on creating a climate where these investors could thrive.

While not all efforts have been equally successful, Singapore deserves credit for its focus on creating a favorable entrepreneurial climate. The list below gives a sense of the range of activities it has sought to encourage[2]:

- Spending for academic research was dramatically increased. For instance, funding at the National University in 2001 was three times the level in 1996. In conjunction with this spending, the government boosted support for entrepreneurial activity at various levels at top universities, from classes for students to incubators to nurture ideas developed by faculty.

- The Agency for Science, Technology and Research not only funds basic research and licenses the output, but reaches out to provide financing to others' "orphan" technologies, as well as subsidies or free consulting advice about commercialization strategies.

- Singapore's enterprise development agency, SPRING, encourages associations that can bring together small and new enterprises for efforts such as training, joint research, and investments in new technologies; it also provides grants for start-ups to hire consultants.

- The Economic Development Board subsidizes part of the research expenses of corporations beginning new initiatives.

- The Techno-preneurship Investment Fund and Singapore's sovereign wealth funds (see chapter 8 for more discussion of these funds) invest in leading global venture funds. While these investors have no special rights or provisions beyond those that other (purely financially motivated) investors receive, these investments help establish relationships that may prove helpful for Singaporean start-ups.

- The Ministry of Manpower and other agencies expedite the paperwork for foreign entrepreneurs interested in beginning a high-growth new business in Singapore.

- A variety of competitions and events with names, such as the BlueSky Festival and Enterprise Day, highlight the potential for new growth enterprises and seek to identify promising nascent entrepreneurs.[3]

One of the most ambitious of these efforts has been the creation of the Biopolis.[4] This seven-building complex, constructed at an estimated cost of $500 million, includes state-of-the-art laboratory facili-

91

ties and other amenities. The nation has aggressively pursued—and lured from institutions as august as MIT, the National Cancer Institute, the University of California, and Kyoto University—top researchers to the Biopolis, offering a combination of state-of-art facilities, generous research funding, stratospheric salaries (reputed to be about $1 million per year), and a favorable political climate. (The latter has been particularly compelling for U.S. researchers, who have frequently expressed frustration with the restrictions on cutting-edge stem cell research that the Bush administration imposed.) By co-locating top-flight researchers, government agencies, and private firms, the government hopes to create the foundation for a vibrant biotech industry in the island-state.

Looking more generally, entrepreneur-enabling efforts can be seen as falling into four broad "buckets":

- Getting the laws right

- Ensuring access to cutting-edge technologies

- Creating tax incentives—or removing barriers

- Training potential entrepreneurs

Getting the Laws Right

The first cluster of policies has focused on ensuring that the legal system supports entrepreneurial activity. Complex contracts abound in the entrepreneurial landscape, most importantly, between firms and their employees, their financiers, and their strategic partners. In the United States, these deals allow very young firms to enter into complex and lucrative arrangements even though the start-up has no history or few assets to speak of.

Efforts to promote entrepreneurship in many nations have focused on duplicating the key aspects of the American system. For instance, over the past fifteen years, the Japanese government has lifted curbs that limited the ability of firms to reward employees with stock options, that restricted the types of stock purchase agreements that investors and entrepreneurial firms could enter into, and that prohibited institutional investors from having assurances that they would not be held responsible for huge losses if a start-up failed.[5] Similar reforms have been taken elsewhere.

The skeptic might argue that these legal restrictions on entrepreneurial contracting may be important in litigious America, but in other nations are simply much less important. While this argument may seem reasonable, backers of the importance of legal rules contend the contracting process is the crucial foundation on which the financing and growth of high-risk, high-return entrepreneurs is built. This argument has been most articulately voiced by Ron Gilson, who is—no surprise!—a law professor:

> Start-up and early stage companies are peculiarly suited to commercializing innovation, yet the character of their organization and the nature of the activity present inherent barriers to their finance. The U.S. . . . manages these barriers and thereby makes early stage financing feasible. The question, then, is whether the U.S. contracting template can be replicated elsewhere: can we engineer a venture capital market?[6]

Gilson relies in his argument largely on historical anecdote (I am of course in no position to throw stones here!), such as the misadventures of nations that have tried to encourage venture activity without having similar legal structures in place. For instance in the German WFG (Deutsche Wagnisfinanzierunggesellschaft) program, the "venture managers" were assured that their losses would be largely covered by the government, limited to modest rates of return from successful investments, and prohibited from controlling the entrepreneurs in which they invested. The program was a miserable failure, generating a return of −25 percent annually.[7]

Large-sample evidence suggests largely the same picture. For instance, an analysis by Antoinette Schoar and myself looks at how the contracts that venture capitalists and the firms in their portfolio enter into vary across developing countries.[8] It highlights the importance of the ability of entrepreneurs and investors to enter into complex contracts, where different outcomes can result if the company's progress varies. (An example would be convertible preferred stock, where the investor can choose either to get back the amount that he or she invested, or alternatively to convert into common stock. In cases where the firm does well, the investor gets all the upside of a shareholder, but has more protection if things get ugly.) Numerous economic theories have suggested that such complex securities are beneficial to all parties concerned, as they allow control over the firm to be transferred to the party that can make the best use of them. In particular, these securities allocate control to the entrepreneur when things are going well, but allow the investors to assert control if the firm is doing poorly. In this way, entrepreneurs can be sure that if they do a good job running the firm, the investors will not be able to use their special rights to wrest away their hard-earned gains.

In the analysis, we show that entrepreneurs and investors in countries with well-defined legal rules and effective court enforcement rely on these complex contracts, in which the assignment of control depends on the performance of the investment. These contracts resemble transactions seen in the United States, which an extensive theoretical literature suggests is an effective contractual solution to the challenges of financing high-growth entrepreneurial firms. By way of contrast, investors in countries with less well-developed laws and courts are far less likely to use convertible preferred stock, and must instead rely on holding majority stakes in firms.

For instance, one group operating in Latin America had initially employed convertible preferred securities in all its transactions. Their enthusiasm for this investment strategy waned, however, when they began litigating with one of their portfolio companies in Peru. The investors found themselves unable to persuade the judge that their preferred stock agreement gave them the right to replace a third-generation founder of the company, even if the group's shares were only convertible into 20 percent of the firm's equity. After this experience, the group structured its subsequent investments as common stock deals in which they held the majority of the equity. In many nations, our interviewees asserted, not only were the entrepreneurs unfamiliar with equity investments that used securities other than common stock, but key actors in the legal system—lawyers and judges—were suspicious and indeed hostile to such transactions. As a result, they forego the benefits of preferred stock.

Again, the skeptical reader might wonder about our claim that these legal structures are important. Just because a structure is used in the United States, is it really ideal everywhere? We found evidence suggesting that these structures really matter, both to the entrepreneurs and the groups that fund them. For instance, when we looked at the valuations assigned to these companies, we found that venture investments in countries with investor-friendlier and better-operating legal systems had higher valuations. To put it another way, to raise a given amount of money, an entrepreneur would have to sell less of his or her company.

Investments in these nations also seem to perform better for the venture investors. Private equity funds that were active in nations with well-operating legal systems had an average return multiple (the ratio of the amount they paid out to the amount they invested) 19 percent better than the typical fund established in that subclass and that year, while those in other countries had a multiple 49 percent worse than the benchmark. Adopting legal structures that are friendlier to new ventures can apparently make a big difference!

Ensuring Access to Cutting-edge Technology
The second set of efforts seeks to encourage the development and transfer of university technologies. Over the past several decades, there have been numerous initiatives around the globe to encourage the commercialization of university technologies. These efforts were ushered in by the United States' Bayh-Dole Act of 1980, which gave universities automatic title to research funded by the federal government and performed at their institutions. (Prior to that, the schools needed to obtain permission to license the technologies from the government, which frequently proved to be a lengthy and uncertain process.) The legislation led to the establishment of technology transfer offices at many schools and a considerable increase in the patenting of academic research.

The *Economist* recently hailed the act as "possibly the most inspired piece of legislation to be enacted in America over the past half-century."[9] (Of course, there are also critics who have been less thrilled

95

with the impact of the law, expressing worries about the consequences for cooperation among researchers, among other issues.) But whatever the concerns, the act has been emulated in recent years in nations from Germany to Malaysia.

Systematic evaluations of legislation to enhance university commercialization remain few and far between.[10] But it seems clear that in many nations, it has historically been extremely difficult to license technologies from research institutions, and that such policy shifts address a real need. Similarly, efforts to build academic centers of excellence—such as the Biopolis described above—have had real success when they are realistic in targets and designed with thoughtful incentives that meet the real needs of researchers. (However, see the cautionary tale of Malaysia described below.)

At the same time, cautions have emerged from the experience of some nations with technology transfer, particularly efforts that have involved raising substantial funds to finance academic spin-outs.[11] Numerous schools and governments have been tempted to consider the establishment of funds that would duplicate the activities of independent venture funds. Case studies and empirical evidence raise doubts about whether such efforts are likely to be successful. In some cases, the academic funds have crowded out independent venture capitalists, discouraging the involvement of individuals who would have the ability to add tremendous value to the spun-out entities. In other cases, these funds have been plagued by poor decision-making, putting many millions of dollars into unsustainable companies:

- Boston University's venture capital subsidiary invested in a privately held biotechnology company founded in 1979 by scientists affiliated with the institution. As part of its initial investment in 1987, the school bought out the stakes of a number of independent venture capital investors, who had apparently concluded after several financing rounds that the firm's prospects were unattractive. Between 1987 and 1992, the school, investing alongside university officials and trustees, provided at least $90 million dollars to the private firm. (By way of comparison, the school's entire endowment at the fiscal year in which it initiated this investment was $142 million.) While the company completed an initial public offering, it encountered disappointments with its products. At the end of 1997, the University's equity stake was worth only $4 million.[12]

- The University of Chicago launched the ARCH initiative in 1987 to encourage commercialization of its own technology and that of Argonne National Laboratory, a federal facility it managed.[13] The group was given a mandate both to license technologies to established firms and to fund start-ups. The venture fund enjoyed some modest initial successes. Shortly thereafter, however, the relationship between ARCH and the University of Chicago was restructured. The ARCH partners received permission to raise a second, more substantial venture fund with far more generous compensation for the venture capitalists. As part of the new effort, they were allowed to invest outside the University, while retaining a formal "right of first look" at the University's technology. ARCH rapidly expanded after raising the second fund, and the share of new transactions originating from the University of Chicago and Argonne fell dramatically. Meanwhile, many at the school believed that in their eagerness to become established as venture investors, the ARCH partners had neglected the more mundane—but necessary—technology-licensing activities.

Relatively few academic-based funds have reached maturity, and data on their activities are limited to case studies of a number of programs. But the difficulties that the pioneering funds have faced—as well as those encountered by their closely related cousins, the corporate venture fund—lead to a dubious prognosis.

Creating Tax Incentives

A third focus has been tax policy. Despite what the previous discussion might suggest, not all entrepreneurs come from academic institutions. Indeed, research[14] suggests that the nearly half the founders of venture-backed firms in the United States were working previously at publicly traded companies. In a classic work, Jim Poterba argued that decreases in capital gains tax rates might increase the attractiveness of becoming an entrepreneur precisely because of such individuals.[15] He argued that increasing the differential between the tax rates on capital gains and ordinary income would spur corporate employees to found companies, thereby increasing the need for venture capital. Paul Gompers and I empirically find support for Poterba's capital gains tax rate claim: lower capital gains taxes appear to boost venture capital fund-raising.[16] The cuts in the capital gains rate seem to have a particularly strong effect on the amount of venture capital supplied by tax-exempt investors, who are not affected directly by the change. This suggests that the primary mechanism by which capital gains tax cuts affect venture fund-raising is by increasing the demand of entrepreneurs for capital. The limited research done in Europe suggests similarly that entrepreneurial activity is sensitive to capital gains tax rates.[17]

Thus, tax policy changes may also directly affect the willingness of investors to supply capital. Rather than cutting all capital gains taxes, one approach that has been employed in many countries is to create special tax rates for capital gains from investments in entrepreneurial firms. For instance, in the United States, noncorporate taxpayers (including partnerships and other entities) may exclude 50 percent of any gain from stock in qualifying small businesses that has been held for more than five years. (As a result, the marginal effective tax rate on capital gains from the sale or exchange of such stock is 14 percent rather than the customary 28 percent, though the presence of the Alternative Minimum Tax may lead to taxpayers paying at a rate between these two levels.) Similarly, in the United Kingdom, to improve the fiscal environment for entrepreneurs and venture capitalists, effective capital gains tax rates on the disposal of business assets held for more than two years have been reduced from 40 percent to 10 percent.[18] Given the evidence on the effectiveness of capital gains tax cuts, but the very real revenue needs that many governments face, such targeted measures may represent an attractive middle road.

If taxes make it costly to succeed as an entrepreneur, other policies—especially common in Europe—punish failure. Another set of initiatives to boost entrepreneurship, then, addresses policies that make it costly to fail. In light of the experiential nature of the entrepreneurial process, policies that punish individuals who are involved with failed ventures can be counterproductive.[19] In recent years, nations such as France, Italy, and Switzerland have lifted punitive legal sanctions that they historically imposed on managers and even nonexecutive directors of bankrupt firms. Singapore has gone even further, and sought to lift the *social* sanctions against failure by establishing the Phoenix award, which annually rewards a tenacious entrepreneur who has overcome an initial failure.

Training Entrepreneurs

A final set of policies seeks to better prepare entrepreneurs by providing education. These policies have taken a variety of forms, from general training to hands-on assistance with the development of business plans. One common model, for instance, is inventors' assistance programs, organizations that help inventors evaluate their proposed products or services before they are introduced. These initiatives typically help the inventor make a more informed decision on whether to pursue an idea, as well as providing background information on financing and strategic routes frequently chosen by entrepreneurs. One estimate is that there are 150 of these centers in the United States alone. Entrepreneurial training programs more generally have been launched in at least thirty nations.[20]

There has been little systematic evaluation of these programs, which are challenging to study because the individuals selected for them are typically particularly promising entrepreneurs. But the work that has been done, in very different settings, paints a positive picture of the benefits from these interventions. Thomas Åstebro and coauthors examine the Canadian Industrial Innovation Centre's Inventor's Assistance Program.[21] In this program, entrepreneurs paid a modest fee to get recommendations on the potential of their idea. The researchers examined the amount spent to develop the idea and its potential returns, as well as what would have happened had entrepreneurs not gone to the Centre for an assessment. The analysis suggested that expenditures on this program have a very attractive rate of return to society, estimated to be between 36 percent and 70 percent annually. But this analysis depends critically on the authors' assumptions about what

99

would have happened in the alternative universe where the entrepreneurs did not get advice from the Centre. In particular, if contrary to the authors' assumptions, entrepreneurs would have soon figured out that their ideas weren't viable even without this consultation, or if bad advice from the Centre discouraged some inventors with great ideas from pursuing them, the results of the analysis could differ markedly.

A very different setting is examined by Dean Karlan and Martin Valdivia, who look at one of the best-known and respected programs that teaches business skills to low-income entrepreneurs.[22] The authors worked with the Foundation for International Community Assistance in Peru, an organization that provides microfinance for poor, female entrepreneurs. Here, the authors were able to run a control: some groups simply met weekly and provided credit and collected repayments, while in others, the meetings also included mandatory training classes. Among the topics covered were competitive strategy, marketing approaches, accounting, and finance.

When the authors surveyed the participants in the classes and the control groups, they found several effects. The class attendees reported engaging in some of the exact activities that were taught in the program, such as maintaining records of sales and expenses and thinking proactively about new markets. Their firms also may have enjoyed greater sales and profits. Interestingly, the greatest impact appears to be had on those members of the lending circles who initially had the least interest in participating.

Increasing the Venture Market's Attractiveness

A second set of policies has sought to increase the attractiveness of the venture capital market to institutional investors. To be sure, steps to boost the attractiveness of entrepreneurship, as described above, are likely also to lure venture funds. But these efforts are frequently different, as they tend to focus on features that international investors, rather than local entrepreneurs or domestic sources of capital, regard as most important.

This assertion might seem surprising. After all, should not local investors be the most inclined to invest in the domestic market? For instance, an extensive body of academic work suggests there is a home bias for investors: we are more comfortable investing in a firm in our hometown than in one across the country, much less across the world.

But there are two countervailing considerations, which suggest why relying just on local investors is often not enough:

- *The relative sizes of the markets.* Given the highly dispersed nature of the world's capital, there will be far more capital outside a given nation than inside. Even a very modest allocation to venture capital on the part of global investors will swamp a more significant domestic allocation in all but a few nations.

- *The greater sophistication of global investors.* In most markets with poorly developed venture capital industries, institutional investors have had very limited exposure to the asset class. Meanwhile, major pension funds, funds-of-funds, and government investment corporations have been investing in this asset class for decades. Over the years, they have developed an understanding of what makes an effective venture capital group, and the confidence to make major commitments when a group satisfies their criteria.

As a result, many of the recent success stories, such as Israel and Singapore, have had the growth of their venture capital industries driven not by inexperienced domestic investors, but global players. In these cases, only after the markets had been validated by global players did local investors begin playing a significant role.

Allowing True Partnerships

At the same time, however, interesting global investors in one's market can pose significant challenges. Foremost among these is ensuring that local and national tax and partnership laws are in complete compliance with what has emerged as the global de facto standard.

In particular, limited partnerships have two features that make them particularly attractive to potential institutional investors:

- *Limited liability.* The "limited" in limited partnership refers to the fact that the outside investors (limited partners) can lose no more money than the amount they put into the fund. Consider a case where a pension invests a million dollars in a venture fund, which invests in a biotechnology company whose experimental drug unfortunately ends up having fatal complications during a clinical trial. The relatives of the victims can sue the company, its leaders, and the venture capitalist for various damages. These would include the wages the victims would have earned, compensation for their pain and suffering, and perhaps punitive damages if the firm and the venture capitalists were negligent, and might total many millions of dollars. But the pension fund can lose no more than the million dollars it originally invested, even if the venture capitalists cannot pay off all the judgments against them and declare bankruptcy. This protection gives institutions much more comfort in making high-risk investments.

- Tax flow-through. Essentially, a limited partnership is "invisible" for tax purposes. Rather than the partnership facing levies, the individual partners are taxed as if they had made the investments themselves. This distinction may sound minor, but it has a great deal of importance to tax-exempt institutions, which make up much of the pool of venture investors: university endowments, pensions, and government funds typically do not need to pay taxes on their investment profits. If taxes need to be paid at the partnership level, these institutions would end up having paid taxes on their investment gains in any case. These provisions also typically allow partners who are taxable to use the losses in the early years of venture funds (when companies have typically not gone public and are still losing money) to offset gains elsewhere, thereby reducing their tax burden.

Indeed, a considerable number of nations, from Japan to Germany, have shifted the ways in which government treats venture capital funds to become more aligned with the approach in the United States. Such shifts are in fact a necessity. Most venture capital investment groups are relatively leanly staffed, and do not have the time or patience to understand the complexities of an idiosyncratic national system. Nations that have had such systems have found it extremely difficult to attract institutional investments to their venture funds, even if the opportunities for attractive returns are substantial.

One illustration of this point is New Zealand. As we'll discuss in the next chapter, the government put into place in 2002 a well-designed program, the New Zealand Venture Investment Fund, to encourage the formation of capital pools to invest in early-stage businesses. Within a few years, the funds had initial successes, but still most global institutions were reluctant to invest in New Zealand funds. Essentially, the funds were only able to raise money from wealthy individuals, corporations, and local financial institutions.[23] In a study David Moore, Stuart Shepherd, and I conducted, we interviewed investors and found that almost all of them had some motivation other than financial returns. Local financial institutions often cited a desire to "give something back" by helping along this local effort; the corporations noted their interest in a obtaining a "window" on some intriguing new technological area; and the individuals mentioned some sort of personal connection, such as a Kiwi friend or a earlier holiday in the country.[24]

One of the reasons for the Venture Investment Fund's inability to interest pensions and other financial investors lay in the lack of a limited partnership structure. While the leaders of the venture development efforts realized early on that this lack was a major problem, they were unable to get key tax officials to understand the magnitude or urgency of the problem. Not only did absence of a limited partnership structure raise questions in the minds of investors about their liability, but it also created tax headaches: the New Zealand tax code taxed partnership profits at the fund, rather than limited partner, level. Investors would thus be facing taxes on their capital gains—even though they were tax-exempt. This feature was a "deal killer" to most.

In 2008, eight years after the inception of the venture initiative, the New Zealand government adopted a limited partnership bill, which brought the nation into compliance with worldwide standards. It is still too early to tell whether this change will trigger a surge of money into the Kiwi venture market—the challenges of a small market far

103

away from major financial centers remain—but without it, there would have been very little chance.

Creating Local Markets

There are other steps that can specifically help ensure the comfort of venture investors. One of them is enhancing local markets for publicly traded firms, so that there are nearby opportunities to take venture-backed companies public.

One of the great fears of venture capitalists when considering deals in emerging markets is that the investments will be difficult to exit: it's a hotel you can check into, but never leave! Public markets are important to entrepreneurs as well. As much as they may appreciate the capital and advice that venture investors provide, entrepreneurs fiercely value their independence. Unless there is some assurance that the venture investors will eventually be able to exit, they are much less likely to get involved in the first place.[25]

During the 1990s, it was commonplace to dismiss these concerns. The presumption was that good technology companies could be readily taken public on the NASDAQ market in New York. But as the barriers to public offerings in the United States have apparently risen, the share of offerings by young firms in the American market has waned. (Whether this pattern is owing to the Sarbanes/Oxley corporate governance reforms, the efforts to curb dubious practices by analysts at investment banks, or the broader changes in the world economy, can be the subject of a fascinating debate, but one that would take us too far afield.) Whatever the cause, a healthy local stock market for growth firms is more important than ever.

The experience of India, which has experienced a spectacular growth in venture capital activity in recent years, is a case in point. The amount of capital invested in young and growing firms exploded from $570 million in 2001 to $3.8 billion in 2007, much of it driven by American, European, and Middle Eastern capital. In addition to the robust growth that characterized the nation and the well-trained workforce, venture capitalists were lured by the robust public markets that characterized India until the beginning of 2008. For instance, in September 2008, 4,917 firms traded on the Bombay Stock Exchange, with 225 new listings in the past thirty-two months.[26] In fact, in many instances, venture capitalists invested in companies that were already publicly traded, and nurtured them while their market value grew and they could achieve a profitable exit. While this market is far from an efficient one, and suffered substantial losses during the financial crisis, it is an important asset for India's entrepreneurs.

The most compelling illustration of the power of the public markets was Warburg Pincus's experience with Bharti Televentures.[27] Between 1999 and 2001, Warburg invested $292 million for eventual ownership of 18 percent of the mobile telephony firm. At the start of the process, the company had 104,000 subscribers, two cellular licenses and one landline license, and a market capitalization of $100 million, while India had a total of 3.6 million cell phone users. Bharti used the investment to acquire three companies, win bids for fifteen licenses, and expand its existing operations, bringing its market capitalization to an estimated $1.5 billion. It went public in January 2002. In March 2005, Warburg sold 6 percent of its Bharti position for $560 million in a highly publicized block trade executed on the Bombay Stock Exchange in twenty-eight minutes. By the time Warburg sold its final stake to the British firm Vodafone in October 2005, Bharti's market capitalization was $15 billion, and observers estimated Warburg's total realizations at $1.6 billion.

Support for the idea that robust local markets are critical comes from the work of Leslie Jeng and Philippe Wells.[28] Looking at the evolution of venture activity over time in twenty-one countries, they found that a robust market for public offerings was a critical driver of venture activity. The number and size of IPOs affect the amount of venture capital invested. Interestingly, early- and later-stage venture capital investments are affected quite differently by the determinants of venture capital: IPOs explain less of the year-to-year fluctuations in early-stage than in later-stage investments. Presumably, while early-stage firms, being unlikely to complete an IPO for a few years, are still somewhat removed from the public markets, later-stage investors are keenly aware of and affected by the market's ebbs and flows.

It should be noted that establishing small-capitalization markets can be a tricky endeavor. The experience of the European Venture Capital

105

Association is illustrative. After the October 1987 decline in world equity prices, IPO activity in Europe dried up, as it did in the United States.[29] But unlike the United States, which recovered with a "hot" IPO market beginning in 1991, in Europe there was no recovery. In 1992–93, there were 432 IPOs on the NASDAQ; on European secondary markets (which had only 30 percent of the number of firms listed in the United States to begin with), there were only 31. In some countries, the decline in IPO activity was even more extreme: only five companies listed in Germany's two secondary stock markets in 1992–93; none listed in Denmark's between 1989 and 1993. Consequently, European private equity investors found IPOs of firms in their portfolios to be much more difficult to arrange, and were more likely to exit firms through the sale of firms to third parties. Trading volume in European markets for small-capitalization firms had also lagged.

One response to these problems was the creation of the EASDAQ market.[30] The European Venture Capital Association envisioned EASDAQ as a pan-European public market for growing companies—modeled after the liquid and generally efficient NASDAQ market in the United States. But despite a huge investment of time and energy, EASDAQ was a miserable failure: only several dozen firms listed on the new exchange after its launch in 1996.

In part, this failure reflected a classic catch-22: because there was so little trading on EASDAQ, it was extremely difficult and costly to get into or out of positions there. These costs deterred firms from listing on the market, which perpetuated the market's lack of liquidity. But there were other problems as well. Foremost, EASDAQ soon attracted competition from a variety of European nations, which desired that the preeminent European market for small-capitalization stock be situated in their own nation. Many national exchanges reestablished or upgraded their second-tier markets. This competition led to a "race to the bottom," in which EASDAQ was forced to lower its initially lofty listing standards and admit some rather dubious companies to try to establish itself as the leading exchange. These mishaps only further tarnished EASDAQ's luster. (Though, in fairness, it should be pointed out that EASDAQ never reached the depths of the roughly contemporaneous American effort to create a small-firm stock market, the American Stock Exchange's Emerging Company Marketplace. This exchange was distinguished by listing a fire-protection company headed by a convicted arsonist and another firm whose gender-bending CEO had previously been banned twice from the securities industry, once while a man and once as a woman.)[31] Ultimately, the European exchange was acquired and then ignominiously shut.

Accessing Human Capital Abroad

Another "venture capital stage setting" response involves leveraging human resources outside the nation. Venture capital is a true "people business" where personal connections are critical to overcoming the very substantial information gaps that surround these risky investments. Thus, it is not surprising that ties to entrepreneurs and venture investors working in more developed markets can often be critical.

Most countries have large pools of expatriates, which often include many individuals active in high-technology and venture capital industries abroad. These people can serve as a valuable resource along several dimensions, including roles as angel investors, as mentors to, or even partners of, local venture capitalists, and as sounding boards for policymakers.

The nation that has probably benefited the most from this resource has been India, particularly from the substantial Silicon Valley community of first- and second-generation Indians. India has an extensive diaspora, estimated to total 18 million people in 130 countries, many of whom are highly skilled.[32] As a result, they serve as a very valuable resource to local entrepreneurs: Annalee Saxenien found that two-thirds of the Indian-born entrepreneurs working in Silicon Valley advised entrepreneurs in India, while 18 percent invested in those firms.[33]

Indeed, Tarun Khanna and Ramana Nanda found that these contacts are especially valuable for Indian entrepreneurs located outside the major centers of software development.[34] Because the leaders of these firms do not have as many peers to learn from, and presumably find it harder to attract potential venture investors, contacts with seasoned entrepreneurs in other nations can be valuable. Khanna and Nanda found that firms with these contacts performed considerably better than others in their region, an effect that is weaker for the firms located in entrepreneurial hubs, where presumably these key inputs are more readily available.

While the Indian government has tried to encourage such ties—for instance, recruiting prominent expatriate entrepreneurs to various advisory panels—many of these connections have happened more serendipitously. Other countries have employed more aggressive efforts to catalyze these flows of knowledge and capital: for instance, in 2000, Singapore opened an office in California called connect@sg, which, among other things, sought to reach out to Singaporeans working in Silicon Valley and connect them with native entrepreneurs.[35]

A natural concern with all these steps to make raising capital from global investors easier is the danger of losing the firms. If entrepreneurs receive capital from foreign investors, they may list overseas and subsequently move their headquarters and ultimately their operations overseas. Indeed, many pioneering high-growth companies of the 1990s did get drawn inexorably to the United States, as part and parcel of listing on the then-dominant NASDAQ market. Today, the emergence of viable exchanges elsewhere has reduced this problem, but firms continue to move to more fecund territories.

But the experiences of many nations over the past decade suggest that even if such defections do occur, the success of an entrepreneurial company still has many positive effects on the country where it began. These include

- the encouraging effect that the example has on would-be entrepreneurs,

- the visibility that the firm—and local companies more generally—gain with global investors (thus encouraging further investment), and

- the likely continuing involvement by the transplanted entrepreneur with the local economy as a mentor to entrepreneurs or an angel investor.

108

FINAL THOUGHTS

In their eagerness to jump-start entrepreneurial activity, governments frequently race to hand out capital. This is equivalent to serving the main course before setting the table, and unlikely to lead to a successful dinner party.

This chapter has emphasized the importance of steps that help entrepreneurs and facilitate global investors. Failing to focus on creating favorable conditions for entrepreneurs will lessen the demand for the funds that are made available. And if global investors do not find conditions attractive, the experience and sophistication needed to create a world-class venture industry are unlikely to be present.

This brings us to the final category of policies: direct interventions to increase the supply of capital for entrepreneurs and venture capitalists. These efforts have differed along many dimensions:

- *The parties providing the capital.* In many instances, government officials have handed out the funds themselves. In others—aware of the distortions that can creep in—academic institutions or nonprofits have been delegated to provide the funding. In yet others, private sector organizations have been provided capital to give in turn to entrepreneurs.

- *The amount of funding.* In some cases, the public bodies have provided matching funds only; in others, the entire amount needed has been provided.

- *The structure of the funding.* In some cases, the funding has been in the form of outright grants; in other cases, governments have expected to receive their capital back or a return on their investments.

- *The "strings" attached to the capital.* The extent to which the government contracts have constrained the activities of these firms and funds has varied substantially.

- *The relationship between the government and the firm or fund receiving the funding.* In many cases, the government has few mechanisms in place to oversee the group once the capital has been provided; but in others, there is much more intensive monitoring.

Direct interventions present far more substantial challenges to public officials than the previous two types of initiatives we have looked at. There is always a danger of spending public resources unwisely: for instance, a tax subsidy for capital gains may not generate enough economic activity to make up for the revenue loss. But the pitfalls are considerably larger as the government moves from "scene setting"—from policies that facilitate the demand for venture capital—to directly providing capital itself. In the next two chapters, I will highlight the several challenges that policymakers face, and the disasters to which, far too often, poorly designed programs have led.

CHAPTER 6

HOW GOVERNMENTS GO WRONG: BAD DESIGNS

The frequent failures among public programs to stimulate entrepreneurship and venture capital suggest that many pitfalls face these efforts. The stark truth is that many more initiatives have been unsuccessful than successful. One benefit that policymakers today have, however, is that they can learn from the mistakes made in earlier years, and adjust their programs accordingly.

Readers may wonder how this book's recommendations have been arrived at, given my cautions about the early stage of our knowledge. Indeed, not enough work has been done on how to structure entrepreneurship programs to ensure their greatest effectiveness and to avoid political distortions. But as I discuss later in this chapter, a number of previous programs appear to be predicated on premises that are fundamentally at odds with what is known about the process of financing entrepreneurial firms.

The next two chapters will highlight the critical challenges these initiatives face, drawing on research and history. In this chapter, we'll look at conceptual problems. All too often, public programs incorporate fundamental errors that are a death sentence for a program before it even starts. These failings can be divided into designs that do not reflect what the entrepreneurial and venture process is all about, and those that seek to tell the market what to pursue, rather than listen to its needs. In the chapter 7, we will consider some of the key errors made when programs are implemented.

Failing to Understand the Venture Market

If public programs are indeed to create an environment in which new ventures can succeed, they must first understand the ways in which the market identifies and funds high-risk, high-potential entrepreneurs. All too often, programs have incorporated assumptions that may have sounded plausible when proposed within the halls of government but are utterly at odds with the manner in which venture markets really work.

In this section, I will highlight three common ways in which public efforts misunderstand the working of venture markets.

Timing

The first common mistake relates to the length of the programs. Democracies worldwide are shaped by the ebb and flow of election cycles. This inevitably leads to a short-run orientation. And even leaders in office for life are often anxious to display progress and look for quick fixes.

But building a venture capital industry is a long-run investment, which takes many years until tangible effects are realized. To cite one example, historians date the birth of the modern U.S. venture capital industry to 1978, a full twenty years after the enactment of the SBIC program. (The gestation period in the United Kingdom was even longer.) While it may be possible to build a vibrant entrepreneurial sector more quickly today (as we will discuss below, the globalization of the industry has some dramatic implications), this is not a process that can be accomplished in a few years.

As a result, an entrepreneurship or venture capital initiative requires a long-run commitment on the part of politicians and public officials. The one certainty is that there will be few immediate returns. If programs are abandoned after a few months or years, they are highly unlikely to bring any benefits. There has to be a commitment to be undaunted by initial failures—for example, the low rate of return that early publicly subsidized investments or funds garner—and instead to fine-tune programs in the face of early discouragements.

An illustration of the need for commitment is the experience of Malaysia. To their credit, Malay policy leaders recognized early on the importance of encouraging entrepreneurial activity. In the 1970s, Malaysia began its transition into a middle-income country by gradually broadening its economic activities and switching from the production of raw materials, such as rubber and palm oil, to the manufacture of electronics. By the early 1990s, the nation's leaders recognized that Malaysia's future growth depended on encouraging innovation.

In 1993, the Malaysian Industry-Government Group for High Technology (MIGHT) was launched. This independent, nonprofit organization aimed at facilitating partnerships between industry and government in high-technology industries. It became an active advocate for efforts to promote high-technology entrepreneurship: for instance, the Multimedia Super Corridor, encompassing an area of nearly 300 square miles, was started in 1995 and was explicitly modeled after Silicon Valley.[1] The importance of this effort was reflected in the comments of the most senior levels of the Malay government: for instance, in 1999, Tan Sri Dr. Omar Abdul Rahman, the joint chairman of MIGHT and president of the Malaysian Academy of Sciences, pointed to the success of Singapore in promoting high-technology entrepreneurship and argued that there was a "need for a paradigm shift."[2] This vision was largely incorporated into Malaysia's five-year plans in the late 1990s and 2000s.

However worthy the initial vision, its implementation was marked by inconsistency that largely defeated the government's good intentions. Consider, for instance, the efforts in biotechnology.[3] In 2001 the Malaysian prime minister, Mahathis Mohamad, set in place plans to boost Malaysia's biotechnological capacities through the establishment of a BioValley: Malaysia targeted biotechnology (like almost everyone else!) as critical to the nation's development. The BioValley itself was intended to nurture local research and medical discoveries and enhance commercialization. At the core of the 2,000-acre site would be three research institutes focusing on genomics and proteomics, agriculture, and pharmaceutical technologies, which would share resources. The valley was projected to be fully operational in 2009, and would also have commercial, education, recreation, and residential facilities, with a total public expenditure exceeding $150 million.

Inauspiciously, the BioValley was built on the site of Entertainment Village, Malaysia's failed attempt to create a version of Hollywood. Reflecting the absence of advance planning or follow-through, this expensive real estate development lay empty. In an echo of the earlier failure, by April 2004 only three companies had signed contracts to locate in the BioValley, and by 2005 the empty halls of the BioValley and unused equipment had earned the place the nickname the "Valley of Bio-Ghosts."

What went wrong with this effort? In part, it reflected the lack of planning highlighted above. Perhaps blinded by the success of Singapore's Biopolis, the Malaysia effort's leaders apparently did not ask whether biotechnology firms wanted to locate in the BioValley. The lack of properly trained talent to operate research facilities, the uncertain nature of intellectual property rights in Malaysia, and the absence of a national tradition of high-technology entrepreneurship all weighed heavily in the mind of private firms considering this facility. Rather than engage in dispassionate analysis of the likelihood of attracting tenants, the project's leaders seemed to follow the mantra of the movie *Field of Dreams*: "If you build it, they will come." As we have seen, in the realm of growing venture activity, this strategy is rarely enough.

The inconsistencies of Malaysian policies also led many biotechnology firms to turn elsewhere. For instance, not long after breaking ground on the center, the Science, Technology and Environment Ministry announced the establishment of biotechnology satellite hubs in all of the country's states by 2006, with each state concentrating on a particular scientific field.[4] These changes, as well as the shroud of secrecy under which the project was organized, led many to wonder about the government's commitment to BioValley. (This kind of push to be "fair," to ensure that every region gets a "piece of the action," has defeated many similar efforts.) Then, in April 2005 the nation's biotechnology policy was revisited. The plans for the BioValley were scaled down, in favor of institutes elsewhere and focused on other industries, tax breaks, and matching incentives.

Perhaps not surprisingly, firms participating in other Malay programs also saw dizzying changes of policy and inconsistencies, which reduced their effectiveness. For instance, the Advanced Microchip

Design and Training Center project was launched in 1999, with a vision of establishing fifteen semiconductor design houses employing 5,000 designers by the end of 2003.[5] An important element was to be intensive training of local students to prepare them for state-of-the-art work. The government enthusiastically supported this effort, pointing to its fit with the broader goal of promoting information technology. But by 2003, the government—apparently discouraged at the slow pace of progress—had largely abandoned the project, and ended up in litigation with its various foreign partners. Similarly, the Malaysian Technology Development Corporation underwent numerous shifts of strategy in the face of severe write-downs, continuous losses from 1999 to 2004, and corruption charges against its most senior executive.[6]

This experience is not unique to Malaysia. A recent evaluation by Scott Wallsten looked at counties in the United States that had been the site of publicly funded science parks, and compared them to similar counties that did not have such facilities.[7] An initial comparison suggested that science parks had little impact: for every park such as the Center for Advanced Technology at Colorado State University, which saw a surge in venture funding in the years after its establishment, there is a Alturas Technology Park, in Moscow, Idaho, where the growth rate in high-technology employment and venture activity in the five years after it was built lagged behind that of peers without such a park.

It might be objected that this comparison isn't really fair. After all, in many cases, a key reason that the government decides to spend precious public funds on these projects is that the area is in trouble economically to begin with. Not surprisingly, science parks tend to be located in counties that are losing jobs. But even after controlling for economic conditions, the basic pattern remains: these parks have no measurable impact, positive or negative, on venture activity or high-tech jobs more generally.

Much of the blame for the failures of these parks must be laid at the feet of the short-run orientation of many government leaders. All too often, leaders assume that a science park project, once completed, will solve problems immediately. One frustrated park director compared the state legislature—which cut off funding for his center after "not enough had happened" within two years of its opening—to a child who kept digging up the ground where he had planted seeds because he was frustrated that the flower was not yet blooming.[8] A short-term outlook is fundamentally at odds with what we know about the entrepreneurial process.

Even if programs are given a long-run mandate, they are often structured in a way that makes it impossible for them to carry out their mission. Consider, for instance, the experience with promoting entrepreneurship and venture capital in Finland.[9] The Finnish effort has relied on two institutions:

- The Finnish Industry Investment Ltd (FII) was begun in 1995, with the objective of assisting venture funds investing in early-stage companies. It invests directly in these funds, frequently serving as the lead, or cornerstone, investor. It also directly finances entrepreneurs with promising business plans.

- The Finnish National Fund for Research and Development (abbreviated Sitra) has been involved in making government investments in venture capital since 1967. While it originally focused on overseas funds, it also increasingly focused on early-stage funds and in giving money directly to early-stage domestic entrepreneurs.

The overlapping roles of these two agencies might well have given policymakers pause. But these two institutions also shared another, considerably more problematic feature: financial "ground rules" that were inconsistent with their basic missions. On the one hand, FII operated under the rule that its investments be undertaken profitably. This requirement has been interpreted by the bureaucracy as meaning that its returns *each year* were expected to be above the inflation rate. Sitra, on the other hand, was expected to be an "evergreen" fund, with the pace of new investments limited to whatever the fund gets from selling its proceeds.

These requirements seem quite out of line with the funds' ultimate objectives of addressing failures in early-stage venture capital markets. As we have discussed in chapter 2, venture markets are intensely cyclical with booms and busts. This is particularly true of early-stage investing. To expect a steady flow of profits, as the government does from FII, is not realistic. This requirement appears to have led FII to emphasize later-stage investing, in the hope that a more steady profit flow would allow the fund to remain in compliance with its ground rules. Not only is this hope probably ill-founded, but the shift has meant the program has moved away from the mission that the legislators assigned it.

Sitra's requirement of financial self-sustainability has also been counterproductive. In particular, the fund had ample capital to throw into the overheated market of 1999–2000, when the Finnish market was exploding and few entrepreneurs with a decent (or not so sensible) idea were languishing unfunded. By 2001 and 2002, by the time that the Finnish venture market was prostrate, Sitra had no outflows that would allow it to fund anyone.

When enacting these two programs, Finland's parliamentarians realized they needed long-run investments to overcome market failures. But in the design of these programs, seemingly reasonable requirements—who can be against self-sufficiency?—ended up undoing their good intentions. As a result, the ability of these initiatives to address the societal problems that legislators had identified was profoundly compromised.

Given the long span involved in creating a vibrant entrepreneurial and venture capital culture, a short-term perspective (or rules that inadvertently introduce such a point of view) is likely to be a "kiss of death." Political leaders need to appreciate that quick returns are unlikely to appear. If short-term fixes are the only kind of successes being sought, it is best not to undertake a pro-entrepreneurial program at all.

Sizing

The second common mistake relates to the sizing of the program. Either too small or too large an initiative can pose profound difficulties.

The problem with too small a program, of course, is that it won't make much of a difference. For instance, some public programs have only invested a few million dollars. Such an effort is very unlikely to make an impact on a large and diverse economy. Few venture capital-

117

ists or other investors will learn about the program, and the possibility that such funding will serve as a "stamp of approval" to others will be remote. The companies or groups receiving the funds are unlikely to have enough capital to move on to the next level. (While the minimum size varies by country and sector, conversations with practitioners suggest $60 to $75 million is the smallest size for an effective venture fund.)

Yet in many cases, the public sector has created programs that are far smaller.[10] In 1991 Peter Eisinger found that the average size of twenty-nine venture capital programs begun by twenty-three U.S. states was $6.5 million. By way of contrast, the typical venture fund begun that year was $31 million. In many cases, governors and legislators sought to promote the state's economic development, but at the same time to have as little impact as possible on the meat and potatoes of government: funding schools, building roads, and so forth. With such limited money—and often inflated promises about the impact these funds would have—the odds that they would fulfill expectations were remarkably low. Indeed, when Eisinger returned twenty months later to check on the state funds' status, over a third had already been dissolved.

Nor is the creation of too small funds a uniquely American phenomenon.[11] For instance, the European Union has launched numerous efforts to encourage the financing of new firms. Typically, they have followed a depressingly familiar pattern: even if the intention of the Eurocrats is to create reasonable-sized funds, by the time every country, or every region in each country, gets its "fair share" of the government's money, the pie has been sliced in very thin pieces indeed. The European Seed Capital Fund Scheme is one telling example. As Gordon Murray points out, these funds (which typically had under two million euros in capital) were so undercapitalized that even if they did nothing beside pay for the salary of an investment professional and an administrative assistant, rent for a modest office, and travel, and never invested a single dollar, they would run out of capital long before their assigned ten-year life was up. Moreover, with so few euros to disperse, the investments they could make were tiny. Certainly, they were insufficient to get the typical entrepreneurial company to the point where it

118

could go public, or even, in many cases, to the point where it would be interesting to a corporate acquirer. For a number of groups, their best hope of achieving any return from their investments was to sell the stakes back to the companies they had bought them from. This is hardly a way to achieve the European Commission's goal of providing capital to needy entrepreneurs!

On the other hand, if public programs become too large, they can crowd out, or discourage, private funding. Public funds may become so extensive that they discourage venture capitalists from investing in a given market, because all attractive opportunities have been funded already by the public funds.

The experience of the Canadian Labor Fund Program in the 1990s provides a good illustration of this latter danger.[12] A number of provincial governments, seeking to encourage venture capital, established these funds in the 1980s and 1990s. But in doing so, they adopted some very peculiar elements:

- Rather than encouraging institutional investors and sophisticated high-net-worth investors—who are the dominant investors in venture funds around the world—these funds were designed for the "little guy." Individual investors received exceedingly generous tax credits—they received a credit of 20 percent of the amount they invested in these funds when paying their federal taxes, and another 20 percent credit in many provinces—but the benefits were capped after a few thousand dollars.

- Reflecting the political horse-trading that is part and parcel of the democratic process, the Quebec parliament (which enacted the first of these funds and whose legislation was widely imitated in other provinces) decreed that these funds would be managed by labor unions. Predictably, unions were unfamiliar with the venture process, leading to a "rent-a-union" dynamic where outsiders curried favor with unions to get permission to run their funds. Not surprisingly, the unions often turned to cronies and fast-buck operators rather than experienced investors to manage the funds. There were no incentives for the unions to hire top-tier managers,

119

or any provision for government program managers to step in if a problematic manager was hired.

- The funds frequently had wide-ranging, somewhat muddled mandates, which ran from generating financial returns to providing labor education to promoting local economic development.

- Tight limits were put on how long the funds could "sit" on the money they raised. For instance, in Ontario, one-half the funds had to be invested in the first year, and 70 percent within two years, whether there were attractive opportunities or not.

- Numerous costly reporting requirements were imposed on the funds and were compounded by the presence of many individual investors.

Despite these design imperfections, the amount of capital investors put into labor funds grew spectacularly: the investment pool climbed from $800 million in 1992 to $7.2 billion in 2001, while private independent funds grew from $1.5 billion to $4.4 billion over the same period (all figures in billions of 1992 Canadian dollars).

But the funds that were established and raised capital were far from inspiring. For instance, the Canadian Football League Players' Association sponsored the Sportsfund.[13] Joel Albin, a former vice president of the Bank of Montreal, was the leading spirit behind the venture. He candidly described his motivations:

> When I saw what the labor-sponsored vehicle offered with the tax breaks, I thought, "Geez, if I can structure it in a way that I could get my investors those tax breaks, then why not?" It would be sort of negligent not to as a corporate finance person.

This effort attracted so much interest it had to be closed off to new investors. Perhaps the investors were more swayed by the glitzy launch party, which featured the fund's advisors—Canadian professional sports heroes and Olympians—than by Albin's lack of investment experience. But after disappointing investments in such ventures as the

World Pitch & Putt Corporation (which promoted an Irish variant of golf, where no hole is more than 300 feet from the tee) and a short-lived Broadway musical based on *Jane Eyre*, the fund lost more than half its value, and investors fled.

The consequences of this poor design are not surprising. The performance of labor funds lagged far behind both private and public equity indexes in the United States and Canada. The apparent disconnect between poor results and the large amount raised presumably reflected the power of the tax benefits the labor funds enjoyed, as well as uninformed investors.[14]

The effects of the labor fund initiative have been analyzed by Douglas Cumming and Jeffrey MacIntosh.[15] They look at the level of venture capital funding in each province, and see whether the presence of the labor fund program enhanced or reduced the amount of funding. They show that the adoption of the federal legislation seems to be associated with a reduction, not an increase, in overall venture activity. But this analysis raises concerns: in particular, to what extent did the federal legislation coincide with some other change that made Canadian venture investing less attractive than that in the United States (for instance, the proliferation of pioneering Internet companies in California)?

In the second part of their analysis, Cummings and MacIntosh exploit the fact that the program was not begun or ended in all provinces at once: rather, it was phased in and out at various times, reflecting Canada's decentralized government. In this way, they are able to control—at least roughly—for the changing investment climate, and look at the consequences of the adoption of the program specifically. Here the results are indecisive. Certainly there is no evidence that the program boosted the aggregate amount of venture spending in each province.

While this analysis is suggestive, by focusing on the aggregate amount of venture investments, the authors may be missing the larger picture. Conversations with independent Canadian venture funds indicate that they found themselves during these years competing against these uninformed investors, who were in many cases willing to commit capital at huge valuations. Many of the independent groups, con-

121

vinced that they could not generate profitable returns in the Canadian market, shifted (at least temporarily) to investing in the United States instead. Thus, the problem may have been less with the aggregate amount of funding during these years, than with the quality of the groups providing the funding to the entrepreneurs.

Evidence consistent with this view is presented in a recent evaluation of the Canadian program by James Brander, Edward Egan, and Thomas Hellmann, which looks in depth at what happened to individual companies participating in it.[16] The authors find that not only were the companies backed by the labor funds less financially successful, but they underperformed on other measures that might have also been goals of policymakers. The fund-backed firms were less likely to be issued patents or perform R&D, which suggests that they were less innovative than their peers. (The authors control for the fact the tendency of firms in different industries to file for patent protection varies.) Nor is there any evidence that these firms were any better at expanding employment or introducing more competition to Canadian industry, two other justifications that have been offered for the program. In short, by flooding the market with funds, the program appears to have accomplished neither its financial nor broader social goals.

In all fairness to the Canadians, the Labor Fund program was far from unique in having these design flaws. A similar picture emerges from studies of European initiatives. Dozens of national and Europe-wide initiatives in recent decades have sought to promote funding for entrepreneurs and venture capital funds. To cite just one of many examples, in 2001, the European Commission provided more than two billion euros to the European Investment Fund, making it overnight Europe's largest venture investor. This amount is very significant relative to the roughly four billion euros that were invested by European venture funds in that year.

The motivation of these efforts was again laudable. Europe has seen a low level of venture activity for many decades. Figure 6.1 illustrates the ratio of venture investment to gross domestic product for leading industrialized nations, and highlights the low level of activity across Europe.[17] These low levels reflect the miserable returns that European

Percentage

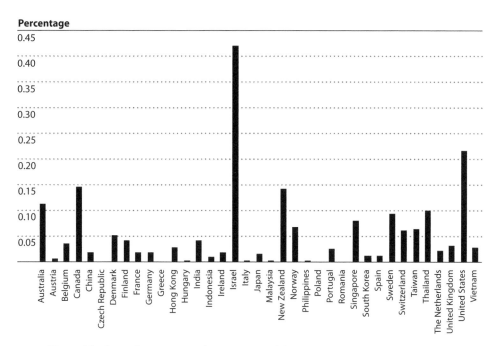

Figure 6.1. Ratio of venture capital investment to GDP, 2007

venture investments have yielded. Venture Economics' calculations suggest that from the beginning of the industry through the end of 2007, the average European venture fund has had an annual return of minus 4 percent: hardly a number to warm the hearts of investors![18] (The comparable number for U.S.-based funds over the same period is 16 percent.) Thus, policymakers have argued, the low levels of fundraising and low historical returns create a need for public financing.

But just as in the Canadian case, the huge amount of funds provided at the European, national, and regional levels may be having a perverse effect. As Wim Borgdorff of the leading European fund-of-funds AlpInvest has noted, "The unfair competition from public money might well have a disastrous unintended consequence by inducing many private funds with stricter financial criteria to leave the European venture capital industry altogether."[19]

Support for this claim comes from a 2006 paper by Marco Da Rin, Giovanna Nicodano, and Alessandro Sembenelli, which examines the level of venture capital funding across fourteen European countries over the past two decades.[20] The authors look at the extent to which venture capital is an important source of financing for private firms. The analyses suggest that many factors determine the level of activity. Particularly harmful are high rates of taxation, the presence of legal hurdles to entrepreneurship, and the absence of stock markets geared toward entrepreneurial companies characteristic of many countries. The supply of funds from the government, however, has no significant impact. Once again, the data suggest that for every dollar being handed out by a government-sponsored program or fund, private investors put a dollar less into the sector. And if the most skilled and knowledgeable investors are on the private side, the quality of investment selection, advice, and oversight in this market may decline markedly as a result of public interventions. To put it another way, the low returns in the European venture markets may be as much a *consequence* as a cause of the massive public interventions in these markets.

This problem is not dissimilar from the difficulties facing the few pioneering venture funds operating in Africa over the last decade. There are so many governmental and quasi-governmental financing sources that would be satisfied with simply getting their capital back that it is next to impossible for private investors to put their funds to work. The relatively few promising entrepreneurs find the venture funds' need for a 25 percent or 30 percent return on their investment unsatisfactory, preferring to take funds from public sources that do not demand a market rate of return. Once again, seemingly well-intentioned public programs can stymie the development of a crucial intermediary. Many other illustrations of this phenomenon, where a publicly subsidized competitor drives out private investment, can be found on other continents as well.[21]

Flexibility
A third point is that government officials must appreciate the need for the flexibility that is central to venture capital investment. Venture capitalists make investments in young firms facing tremendous uncertainties in technology, product market, and management. Rather than undertaking the (often impossible) task of addressing all the uncer-

tainties in advance, they remain actively involved after the investment, using their contractually specified control rights to guide the firm. Changes of direction—which often involve shifts in product market strategy and the management team—are an integral part of the investment process. Far too often, public administrators view these shifts not as natural evolution, but as troubling indications that awardees are deviating from their plan.

The consequences of inflexibility can be seen in the two largest venture programs run in the United States over the past fifteen years. The U.S. Department of Commerce's Advanced Technology Program (ATP) sought from 1990 to 2007 to support technology-based projects conducted by American companies and industry-led joint ventures. In its first eight years, 36 percent of ATP funding went to small businesses, with an additional 10 percent going to joint ventures led by small businesses.

The regulations governing ATP stated that the firms funded be "precommercial." The rationale for this policy was easy to understand: the drafters of the law wanted to support young companies that would find it hard to raise funds elsewhere. But note, demanding that companies be precommercial is very different from encouraging early-stage investing. As numerous scholars of entrepreneurship have pointed out, successful early-stage companies are almost immediately focused on interacting with customers and refining prototype products, despite their young age.[22]

The consequences of the ATP's regulations are not hard to anticipate. For instance, one very promising awardee, Torrent Systems, completed preproduct R&D ahead of schedule.[23] But instead of rewarding the firm, the ATP forced Torrent to choose between giving up the unused money and expanding its R&D into nonessential areas where it did not have commercial activity. Torrent decided to pursue a rapid-commercialization strategy, including an alliance with IBM. ATP promptly impounded the remaining funds. Torrent wasn't anticipating another round of venture financing for a number of months, so its executives now had to scramble to replace the lost financing. All of the events—along with threats from ATP to shut down the company and subject it to an exhaustive audit—consumed immense amounts of Tor-

125

rent's limited time and money. As a result of the government's lack of flexibility, Torrent paid a heavy penalty for its success.

Another example can be drawn from the Small Business Innovation Research (SBIR) program, which sets aside 2.5 percent of all federal external R&D expenditures (the research not directly undertaken by government scientists) to fund small, high-tech businesses. In recent years, the program has invested more than $1.5 billion annually in entrepreneurial technology-intensive firms.[24]

When the SBIR program was enacted, a major concern was ensuring that the awardees would indeed be American-owned small businesses, and not foreign or large companies masquerading as eligible firms. As a result, the legislation required that (*a*) the firms and their affiliates receiving the awards have no more than 500 employees, and that (*b*) the business be 51 percent owned by individuals who were U.S. citizens or permanent residents. These rules governed the program for its first two decades.

In January 2001, however, an administrative law judge deep in the bowels of the Small Business Administration interpreted the law differently, essentially making up a new policy. Companies in which venture capitalists owned more than 50 percent of the equity, the judge ruled, should not be considered as complying with these rules. In particular, because venture capitalists owned a majority of CBR Laboratories of Boston, the firm was not able to receive a SBIR award.

This ruling was profoundly illogical. As we have seen in chapter 3, venture capitalists fund many of the most innovative start-up firms, the bulk of which would now be excluded from the program. Moreover, venture ownership is fundamentally different from the large corporations that the congressmen enacting the program feared would grab the lion's share of the grants: it is a temporary state, as the venture fund is typically required by its operating agreement with investors to sell its stakes within a decade or less of the initial investment. Finally, in many industries, such as biotechnology, raising venture financing is not a choice: the substantial information gaps and intense financing needs mean that sophisticated investors are a necessity. About the only people satisfied with this ruling were hardcore small business lobbyists such as the American Small Business League, who characterized critics of the change as "well-heeled investors [attempting] to hijack billions of dollars in federal contracts earmarked for legitimate small businesses."[25]

As a result, many biotech companies have since been denied SBIR grants or have opted not to apply. We'll never know what would have happened had they been able to pursue their research. In other cases, the effects were more evident, as with Intronn, a Maryland-based company developing a promising therapy for cystic fibrosis by "reprogramming" damaged genes. The firm, started by an unemployed pathologist in his living room, used a grant from the National Institutes of Health to go from three to sixteen employees, as well as to attract venture funding. But when the government learned the firm had sold a majority stake to venture capitalists, it pulled SBIR funding. As a result, the firm had to lay off employees and dramatically scale back its research efforts. It ended the cystic fibrosis project.

In response to the ensuing uproar, the Small Business Administration in 2005 issued a new ruling, which seemed (the language is incredibly opaque!) to allow companies with a majority stake held by venture investors to take part in the program once again, as long as the venture firm itself employs fewer than 500 employees. But the SBA's staffers have continued to do all they can to frustrate the participation of venture-backed firms, apparently convinced that these firms are skirting the rules. One firm's status as a small business was recently rejected, for instance, not because it had too many employees (it had seven), nor because the venture organization funding it did (it had a total of nine employees), but because the sum of the number of employees working for the venture firm and every firm in its portfolio exceeded 500![26] This kind of madness reflects a deep failure in understanding how entrepreneurial finance works.

Inflexibility manifests itself in many ways. One of the international development banks adopted a mandate of trying to boost entrepreneurship in developing countries by investing in the most promising venture funds. As the program evolved, the bank's senior management had a brainstorm: they could better put more money to work, and thus better fulfill their mission, if they co-invested alongside their venture funds in promising companies. This insight translated into a rule that all new investments in funds include a requirement that the bank be offered a chance to co-invest in each investment made.

While once again, the intentions of the policy's drafters may have been innocent, an inflexible policy had troubling consequences. The most sophisticated developing world venture organizations took one look at the policy and decided not to ask the development bank to invest in their next fund. They had no interest in facing the delays, bureaucrat disruption, and loss of flexibility associated with the proposed co-investment mandate. Meanwhile, less successful groups, desperate to raise money at whatever the cost, acquiesced to the mandate. But these were not the funds that the bank was seeking to support! Thanks to an ill thought-through and inflexible mandate, the bank's mission of encouraging the best developing-country-based venture funds was distorted.

In short, public venture capital initiatives should not be hobbled by excessive regulation. However well intentioned, it almost inevitably limits the freedom of venture capitalists and the entrepreneurs they fund to pursue the most attractive opportunities.

Not Listening to the Venture Market

A second problem relates to the way in which public funds are allocated. Far too often, the decisions are distorted by a lack of understanding of how the market works or by political rather than economic considerations. By requiring that matching funds be raised from the private sector, the dangers of uninformed decisions and political interference can be greatly reduced.

We've already seen so many examples of well-intentioned but uninformed leaders making boneheaded decisions that we need not belabor the point! But it is worth saying a few more words about agency problems that can distort public efforts to help entrepreneurs and venture capitalists.

As we noted above, an extensive literature in political economy and public finance has emphasized the distortions that may result from government subsidies as particular interest groups or politicians seek

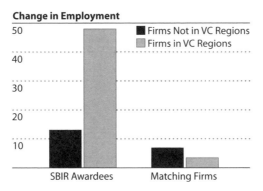

Figure 6.2. Change in employment among SBIR awardees and matching firms

to direct subsidies to benefit themselves. The theory of regulatory capture suggests that direct and indirect subsidies will be secured by parties whose joint political activity, such as lobbying, is not too difficult to arrange.

These distortions may manifest themselves in several ways. One common impetus is the pressure to "spread the wealth": to ensure that every region has its "fair" share of venture subsidies. But as we have seen earlier, entrepreneurship is an intensely unfair activity: there are powerful forces that lead firms to cluster in particular places. Thus, in many cases, much of the impact is diluted as funds that could be very helpful in a core area end up where they aren't useful.

The SBIR program, the largest public venture program in the United States, provides an illustration of this problem. The effect of a fairness policy can be seen by comparing the performance of program recipients with that of matching firms; see figure 6.2, which compares the growth of SBIR awardees and matching firms.[27] The figure shows that the awardees grew considerably faster than companies in the same locations and industries that did not receive awards.

Unfortunately, underneath these positive results lie some intense political pressures and conflicting interests. For one thing, congressmen and their staffers have pressured program managers to award funding to companies in their states. As a result, in almost every recent fiscal year, firms in all fifty states (and indeed every one of the 435 congressional districts) have received at least one SBIR award.

Figure 6.2 also highlights the consequences of such political pressures. In particular, it contrasts what happened to the workforce size of SBIR awardees located in regions characterized by considerable high-tech activity (that is, a firm in the same ZIP code received at least one independent venture capital financing round in the three years before the SBIR award) and those elsewhere.

It reveals that in the ten years after receipt of SBIR funding, the workforce of the average award recipient in a high-tech region grew by forty-seven, a doubling in size. The workforces of other awardees—those located in regions *not* characterized by high-tech activity—grew by only thirteen employees. Though the recipients of SBIR awards grew considerably faster than a sample of matched firms, the superior performance, as measured by growth in employment (as well as sales and other measures), was confined to awardees in areas that already had private venture activity In the name of geographic "diversity," the program funded firms with inferior prospects.

In addition to the geographic pressures, particular companies have managed to capture a disproportionate number of awards. These "SBIR mills" often have staffs in Washington that focus only on identifying opportunities for subsidy applications. This problem has proven difficult to eliminate, as "mill" staffers tend to be active, wily lobbyists. Moreover, "mills" commercialize far fewer projects than those firms that receive just one SBIR grant. Though a *single* SBIR grant does seem to encourage performance in awardee firms, the program clearly still has some work to do in eradicating waste and distortions.

Yet another distortion is when policymakers make decisions based on "buzz," or incomplete information. One study determined that forty-nine of the fifty U.S. states started major programs to promote the biotechnology industry, in hopes of creating a cluster of activity.[28] Realistically, only a handful of these states had the base of scientific resources and the supporting infrastructure (e.g., lawyers versed in biotechnology patent law and financing practice) to support a successful cluster, so the bulk of these funds were wasted. When these programs did support a promising firm, in many cases it rapidly moved to a region more conducive to biotechnology entrepreneurship.[29]

But how, then, can governments be smarter about which sectors to

130

back? This is an especially important goal given that in each new industry there are typically only a few "clusters," or centers of activity. We might be skeptical about whether smart selection is a feasible task for governments, given how little success academics—who have been studying this question for decades—have had in predicting winners. The topic remains actively under research, with little clear consensus. (It is true that there are some clues in the literature: for instance, many observers agree with the conclusions of Lynne Zucker and coauthors, who attempt to disentangle the drivers of the growth of the U.S. biotechnology industry.[30] They argue that the critical element to jumpstart the industry in a given region was the presence of leading academic scientists. Venture funding and the formation of new firms seemed to follow from their presence.)

Certainly, in some instances, government officials have targeted the right sectors at the right time. To cite one example, in just fifteen years, Taiwan moved from having almost no experience in high-technology industries to being a leading producer of hardware for nearly every major computer vendor in the world.[31] Taiwan's success in the computer industry was largely due to a coordinated government strategy to support private entrepreneurship by a large number of small, flexible, innovative companies.

Taiwan's industrial leaders saw that the island was well suited to the international personal computer industry. The open architecture created by IBM in the personal computer (PC) industry lowered the barriers to entry and created a market for standardized components and peripherals. In the earlier mainframe computer era, smaller companies were largely shut out of the market by IBM's market dominance and its strategy of producing a large share of components and peripherals in-house. The PC revolution created a new industry structure, with opportunities for many companies to compete in niches in this fast-growing market. A company could build a better or cheaper component, based on openly available technical standards, and find a buyer for it. Taiwan's leaders also saw that the island's existing industrial infrastructure, which extended from basic parts and components into the plastics, metalworking, chemicals, and electronic industries, would greatly enhance the strength of firms.

131

Taiwan's leaders put in place a government policy that has been aimed at complementing and supporting, rather than replacing, the efforts of the private sector. There has also been an effective flow of information between the public and private sectors. Information from the private sector has enabled government to make policies that address the needs of industry, such as facilitating technology transfer and funding research that the private sector could not afford. Government institutions have provided industry with information on new technologies and market opportunities. Government has also provided for the development of critical human resources needed by industry, emphasizing the production of engineers and computer professionals, the training and certification of existing staff, and the recruitment of high-level, experienced overseas Taiwanese to help develop its information industries.

But Taiwan is the exception rather than the rule. The vast majority of efforts by the public sector to target particular industries seem to have been far less successful. And the academic literature has been not much better in creating workable algorithms to identify which sector is likely to grow at which time. If dozens of Ph.D.s poring for years over econometrics models with mountains of historical data have been unable to show how to target industries, how can the typical government leader identify good prospects in a compressed time period and with limited information?

But there is a way to address this problem at least partially. The most direct way is to insist on matching funds. If venture funds or entrepreneurial firms need to raise money from outside sources, organizations that will ultimately not be commercially viable will be kept off the playing field. In order to ensure that these matching funds send a powerful signal, the matching requirement should involve a substantial amount of capital (ideally, one-half the funding or more should be from the private sector).

An illustration of this approach is the New Zealand Venture Investment Fund (NZVIF).[32] In late 1999 the newly elected prime minister, Helen Clark, realized that New Zealand faced a fundamental problem and needed to change. In particular, she was concerned that New

Zealand's economy depended critically on the production and exporting of commodities. The nation's position in the knowledge-based industries was weak, and its living standards were steadily falling relative to the other major developed nations.

A critical area that her government targeted was enhancing innovation, and encouraging venture capital was a critical aspect of this goal. In light of limited activity in the local market, the government sought to accelerate the growth of the New Zealand venture capital market through co-investment with private investors and related market development activities. After a careful review of other models, the government adopted a so-called fund-of-funds approach, whereby it made investments in private venture capital fund managers (see figure 6.3 for a schematic of a fund-of-funds approach).

Prior to any investments being made, NZVIF was structured as a stand-alone company, which ensured the government could distance itself from risk and liability for the investments made. This approach also ensured distance and independence from decisions about appointment of venture capital fund managers and from individual investment decisions.

These investments were structured as equity (to minimize possible distortions) and could be bought out by the investors. Government investments in the funds were on the same terms as those of private investors, except that each fund was provided with an option exercisable up to the end of the fifth year of the fund to buy out the NZVIF investment on the basis of capital plus interest only (that is, other investors would receive any upside above this amount).

Deliberately, the project's designers asked for no special rights. The fund managers were given responsibility for making and managing investments without government interference. NZVIF leaders participated in investor governance decisions on the same terms as private investors, with the same voting rights. Investor governance arrangements reflected current market practice. The funds were geared toward investors in early-stage companies, and every dollar had to be matched with two dollars from the private sector.

NZVIF's decision to invest in a fund is made following completion

133

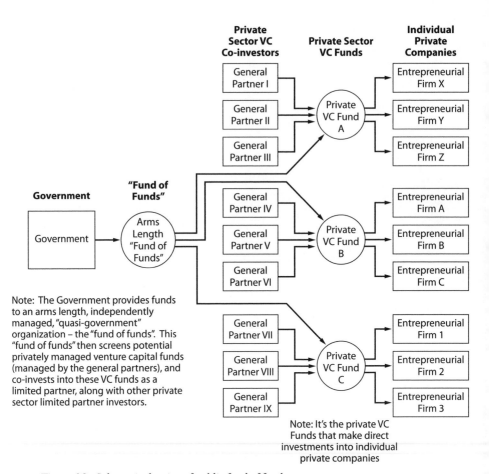

Figure 6.3. Schematic drawing of public fund-of-funds structure

of an extensive selection and due diligence process, undertaken by the fund manager, to determine whether the fund proposal is "investment grade." The initial screening is done by the staff, followed by an outside assessment by an independent specialist private equity advisor. A standard methodology and fixed criteria are used to assess and rank all applications. In many cases, the staff work actively with teams of would-be venture fund managers to help them make their proposals more attractive (for instance, helping them identify prospective additional individuals who can contribute needed experience). This is necessitated by the limited supply of New Zealand–based funds. Following the completion of external due diligence, the NZVIF board selects those applicants with whom it wishes to negotiate investment terms.

As part of the negotiations, a monitoring and reporting framework is agreed with each NZVIF seed fund manager. This enables NZVIF to collect the economic and financial data it needs for the required regular reports on the performance of each fund and the impact of the program. This also enables NZVIF to monitor each fund to ensure it is compliant with its investment agreement and investor governance requirements. Once fund agreements are finalized, investment activity commences.

FINAL THOUGHTS

The provision of public funds to entrepreneurial companies and venture funds is a far trickier process than the "table setting" exercises described in the earlier chapters. Much can go wrong along the way.

But the experience of many programs across the globe suggests some common pitfalls that can be avoided with careful planning. In this chapter, we've highlighted two fundamental challenges that—unless properly addressed up-front—can doom a program before it begins.

The first pitfall is the failure to understand the entrepreneurial and venture capital markets. These markets are complex, and good intentions alone are not enough to overcome fundamental flaws. Any number of poor design decisions—from expecting the effort to bear fruit too quickly, to creating too large or too small a program, to inflexibility in design—can doom an effort.

The second danger is a top-down approach, in which bureaucrats mandate which sectors or locations are to be funded, without listening to what the market is saying. Whatever the motivations for such targeted funding, it is likely to be a road to disaster. Programs are more successful if the entrepreneurs or venture capitalists receiving public funds have to raise matching capital from private sector sources as well. In this way, the market can help sort out which players are likely to succeed, and who will probably be ineffective.

Good design is essential. But the successful implementation of a program also has tricky aspects. These challenges will be our focus in chapter 7.

CHAPTER 7

HOW GOVERNMENTS GO WRONG: BAD IMPLEMENTATION

Even if a program to encourage entrepreneurship is well conceptualized, things can still go wrong once it is begun. The implementation of these programs requires many decisions. While decision making about programs may seem like an obscure, even arcane topic, it is incredibly important. As we'll see from many examples in this chapter, program administrators can make seemingly reasonable decisions that turn out to be destructive.

This chapter will consider three of the most common errors in implementation. Ignoring the need for well-directed incentives, not evaluating what is happening with the program, and failing to allow beneficial internationalization are all mistakes that can be extremely costly, as we will see in the pages that follow.

Not Worrying about Incentives

In addition to providing a clear signal of where the market sees the greatest opportunities (a benefit we discussed in the previous chapter), matching funds have another advantage. If a significant share of the matching funds comes from the managers themselves, they are likely to focus on making sure the investments do well. Yet in many cases, overseers of public entrepreneurship initiatives have not demanded such provisions, and the results have often been disastrous. In particular, the people receiving the funds may adopt a "Heads I win, tails you lose" mentality, which leads to unfortunate outcomes.

Experienced investors in entrepreneurial firms pay an enormous amount of attention to the incentives that entrepreneurs have. For instance, entrepreneurs are frequently forced to accept low salaries—less than they could make in corporate positions. They are not allowed to sell their equity until the investors have liquidated their shares. Other positions that generate income are strictly limited.

One might interpret these restrictions as an indication that well-heeled angel investors and venture capitalists are simply exploiting the entrepreneurs. But their purpose is quite different from mean-spiritedness. The primary concern of investors is ensuring that entrepreneurs "do the right thing": that is, the capital-providers want to ensure that managers take steps that maximize the value of the firm, rather than just benefit themselves. Because it is so hard for even the most diligent investor to oversee all the actions of an entrepreneur, incentives must be correctly aligned. And one of the critical ways to connect the interests of the entrepreneur with that of the firm is to limit the entrepreneur's ability to cash out before anyone else does.

This concern about incentives is seen when it comes to financing venture capital firms as well. Sophisticated investors in venture funds, such as university endowments, make sure that perverse incentives are avoided. For instance, if the venture capitalist is contributing a substantial share of the capital that the fund is raising, and getting rewarded primarily in the form of a share of the capital gains, seasoned investors will likely be comfortable taking part in the fund. Conversely, if the venture team stands to get rich from their management fees whether the investments succeed or fail, the investors will be much less enthusiastic.

Unfortunately, governments have not always thought as carefully about incentives before establishing entrepreneurship and venture initiatives. Far too often, the programs have been designed so that the private sector participants do well, no matter if the investment generates a good return or not. Alternatively, investments may be linked to the fund's financial returns, but not to the broader objectives that motivated the launching of the initiative.

Many examples can illustrate the real danger that the fund managers will have the wrong incentives. The Discovery Fund, for instance, was a $76 million fund organized by New York City in 1995, with

funding entirely from the public sector and public utilities that focused on doing business in the city.[1] The city hired a local venture
group, Prospect Street Ventures, to run the fund, which was launched
with a great deal of fanfare, including Mayor Rudy Giuliani's pledge
that it would generate 4,000 jobs.

Yet the effort is generally regarded as a failure. While the fund did
make some successful investments, such as About.com, many more
were failures. Moreover, several decisions seemed puzzling even at the
time they were being made—such as leading a $14 million financing
round in the web-based broadcaster Pseudo Programs, which was
quickly squandered by the firm (which lacked seasoned management)
before it went belly-up.[2]

Beyond the questionable financial returns, questions were raised
about the extent to which the fund advanced the city's social goals. For
instance, the fund invested in at least two companies not based in New
York City at all. About $3 million was invested in Bondnet Trading
Systems, a Connecticut-based operator of an Internet securities trading service. Bondnet was liquidated, and its assets sold off, in 1997.
Even some of the New York–based investments seemed to have very
limited economic benefits: for instance, the fund's first deal was putting about $2.5 million into Skyline Multimedia Entertainment, an
already publicly traded entity that operated a virtual-reality ride at the
Empire State Building and an arcade near Times Square. The fund
enabled the firm to begin work on a new virtual-reality ride in Sydney,
Australia, a project that soon collapsed. Around the same time, Skyline
Multimedia made substantial loans to one of Skyline's executives.
Within a couple of years, the company was trading at only a few percent of the price at which the initial investment was made—though
not before the Discovery Fund had invested another million dollars in
the firm.

It may have been that at the time of the fund's formation, New York
City–based digital companies—the fund's putative focus—were underfunded. But the bulk of the investments were made during the
bubble period of 1998 through 2000. During these years, local Internet and digital media sector received huge amounts of capital from
independent and corporate venture funds: it is hard to believe that any

kind of market failure was being addressed. Critics wondered whether the compensation scheme worked out for the fund exacerbated the problems. For instance, the *New York Times* noted:

> Among the major beneficiaries of the fund's activities have been the people who run it. Executives at Prospect Street Ventures, the New York-based venture capital firm paid by the city to operate the fund, have also been compensated in cash and stock option grants by companies in which the fund has invested.[3]

It was natural to wonder whether the lack of demand for matching funds and the failure to set a mandate that matched the city's economic development needs intensified the problems that the fund encountered.

An even more extreme example is the Heartland Seed Capital Fund, an initiative by the State of Iowa to spur local activity.[4] The state, seeking to boost venture activity in the region, decided in 1990 to create a $15 million venture fund, which the state's Public Employees Retirement Fund agreed to fund. But rather than looking for a situation where the incentives would be aligned, the retirement fund apparently selected a group in a classic procurement approach: it issued a lengthy request for proposals and waited for venture groups to respond! McCarthy Weersing, a venture group based on the Atlantic and Pacific coasts—but with no experience or personnel anywhere near Iowa—applied and was selected.

Things soon turned ugly. The venture fund charged a hefty management fee of 3 percent per year (between 1 percent and 2.5 percent is more typical for venture funds), but despite the steady fee stream, seemed unable to find any attractive investments to undertake. (The state later pointed out this might have been easier had the venture fund assigned an investment professional to be in Iowa full time. A similar fund in Indiana, which had an active office there, was making a steady stream of promising investments.)

Once again, the incentives were not well thought through. In particular, the venture group got a hefty management fee whether it made investments or not. And indeed, after three years, the fund managers had collected $1.4 million in fees—yet only had made one investment of $1 million. At this point, the fund requested another half-million dollars from the state: not for investments, but to cover its management fees for its fourth year of operations.

The state now suggested that things were not working out and that perhaps the fund should be amicably dissolved. The venture investors, apparently enraged by the loss of their meal ticket, took a far less congenial approach. First, they sold much of the equity in their sole investment back to the management of the company, and used the proceeds to pay themselves the management fee that the state had refused to pay. Then McCarthy Weersing sued Iowa, demanding not just all the management fees that it would have received had the fund remained in business for a decade, as the original agreement proposed, but also for all the profits that would have accrued, had the venture group been able to find and fund successful transactions!

Unfortunately, these experiences are more the rule than the exception. Even programs that appear to be widely accepted as models often have deep design flaws. For instance, Louisiana in 1983 introduced a "CAPCO" (certified capital company) program, in which insurance companies received huge tax subsidies for setting up venture funds.[5] As with the Canadian labor funds discussed in chapter 6, there were few incentives for the insurers to worry about the quality of the managers hired to run the funds, or mechanisms for the public sector to intervene should the investments prove to be flawed. Yet despite these fundamental incentive problems, states from New York to Wisconsin have emulated the structure.

The same sad truth emerges from a systematic study of the performance of almost 7,600 investments in venture capital and buyout funds by institutional investors.[6] Among the questions the study examines is the performance of investments when the investor and the fund are located nearby each other. In studies of *public* markets, a typical finding is that there is "home-field advantage": investors do better when investing in local stocks. Thus, an investor based in Peoria is likely to get better returns from investments in Caterpillar than from those in Komatsu, presumably because proximity brings insights that distant investors don't have.

141

But when we look at venture and other private equity investments, exactly the opposite is true: when putting dollars to work in funds that are nearby, the investor ends up earning returns that are between six and seven percentage points *lower* each year. What can explain this dramatic disparity from the pattern seen in public markets? Shouldn't the added insights from proximity be valuable in this context as well? When we look closely, we see that this surprising result is not a general pattern: it is driven almost entirely by public investors (such as pensions and public university endowments) investing in the state or political jurisdiction in which they are based. Presumably, the fund managers are pressured to help out the region by stimulating local entrepreneurial activity. But these seemingly reasonable requests lead to a lowering of standards and inattentiveness to the investors' incentives, as we saw in the New York City and Iowa examples. All in all, when public authorities channel investment monies to local entrepreneurs and funds, they are following a recipe for mediocre returns.

Clearly, paying careful attention to the incentives offered participants in public programs is essential. Do the entrepreneurs or venture capitalists stand to gain no matter how the investment turns out, as we have seen in some of the examples above? Or do they have a powerful financial stake in the success of the fund? Are the participants driven only to maximize financial returns, or are they steered to address the broader social objectives of the program as well? What if things start going wrong—will they have incentives to stay the course, or instead to behave in a reckless manner? These considerations are critical in the design of investment programs.

THE NEED FOR EVALUATION

Just as venture capital investors carefully analyze the track record of entrepreneurs they are considering funding, government officials should examine the track record of the venture capitalists and entrepreneurs who may receive public funding. Moreover, it is important to look critically at the programs themselves. Far too often, public venture capital programs support underachieving funds and firms. Participants are allowed to linger without a vigorous evaluation.

Evaluations of private sector participants should emphasize two sets of criteria. First, of course, is performance: how well has the fund done to date? But in many cases, evaluating the performance of a venture capitalist or an entrepreneur is not possible until the group has been active for a decade or more.

Thus, it is important to also look at other characteristics that appear to be highly correlated with a participant's ability to achieve its goals. These include the experience of the team, the presence of a clear product market strategy among funded firms, and a strong desire to seek private financing. By devising new methods to search for such factors, government officials would be better able to distinguish between high-performing and underachieving organizations.

For entrepreneurs and early-stage venture capitalists, a limiting factor is experience. A growing body of research suggests that the surest way to be a successful entrepreneur is to have already run a business (hopefully successfully). It thus comes as no surprise that when experienced venture capitalists sink substantial funds in a company, they often place their own handpicked manager in charge. Similarly, there is a lot of "learning by doing" in venture capital: even those venture capital fund managers who may have accumulated business experience as consultants or as members of large organizations are frequently at a disadvantage when compared to those who have invested in young firms before. The successful operation of an early-stage fund can demand very different management skills than those garnered as a consultant or manager. Because much of the know-how needed for guiding and managing start-up companies can be gained only through experience, the presence of entrepreneurs and fund managers who do not have this background can significantly undermine these initiatives' ability to succeed.

Another telltale characteristic of underachieving actors is distractions that undermine their ability to focus on their mission. Legal troubles, for instance, can divert substantial amounts of human and financial resources and even cause dramatic changes in the size and structure of the company. And when an organization is ready to raise more capital, the concerns over pending legal battles often impair the company's ability to attract outside investment dollars.

Research on public programs in a number of nations indicates that another characteristic of underachieving entrepreneurs and venture groups is grants from numerous government sources, with few tangible results to show from previous awards.[7] Because a lack of results can easily be attributed to the high-risk nature of technology development, many organizations are able to avoid accountability indefinitely. These grant-oriented organizations are able to drift from one government contract to the next. Such companies appear to treat public venture capital funds in exactly the same manner as other government research grants: venture-oriented funding neither shows notable returns nor meets unique program goals. While government research grants may be a valuable source of financing to small firms, it is important that they be administered separately, using criteria quite different from venture initiatives.

Adding to the problem is that companies with government grant experience appear to have advantages over other firms when applying for future public awards. Past grants, regardless of project outcomes, help a company gain legitimacy in an area of research, as well as acquire the equipment and personnel needed to do future work. There is also a tendency for some government programs to try to piggyback on other government programs, hoping to leverage their grant dollars. In addition, companies gain insight into the grant application process with each proposal they submit. These organizations consequentially often have a greater chance than others of being awarded government grants. The result can be a stream of government funding to organizations that consistently underachieve.

These performance-undermining factors highlight the need for government officials to critically evaluate each company or fund as a vehicle for accomplishing its goals. This evaluation should go far beyond a simple assessment of the feasibility of a business plan or private placement memorandum. In fact, legal troubles, a long history of government grants, or a lack of germane experience will not even be exposed in the written proposal to the government. It is tempting for evaluators, of course, to attribute the failures resulting from such factors to the high-risk nature of the entrepreneurial process. But to a large extent, organizations exhibiting a high potential for under-achievement can be weeded out by placing a greater emphasis on tell-tale signs during the selection process. The technologies in a venture group's portfolio may be high risk, but the risks of the entrepreneurial team or venture firm itself should be minimized. Regardless of how innovative or enabling a venture capital portfolio may be, if these undermining factors are present, a fund will be hard pressed to succeed.

In sum, research suggests that government officials should closely scrutinize companies and venture funds participating in public programs. Underachieving firms can be weeded out if government officials conduct a comprehensive evaluation of an organization's past performance and examine the tangible progress attributable to previous public funds.

One illustration of the failure to evaluate companies was the experience of Celltech in the United Kingdom.[8] The biotechnology firm was initially funded by the Labour government, which controlled Parliament at the time of the initial investment in 1980. The investment was in part a response to general consternation that the nation was falling behind America in this emerging sector. (These pressures were apparently sufficiently strong that the Conservative Thatcher government, which came to power soon thereafter, acquiesced to the venture.)

Funded initially by the state-run National Enterprise Board, Celltech was also "offered" capital — under government pressure — by a number of leading financial and industrial corporations. The government's Medical Research Council gave the biotechnology company a right of first refusal to license all genetic engineering and related discoveries coming out of the laboratories it ran. This decision was widely seen as a way for the Council to diffuse criticism about its track record in the 1970s, when its laboratories made some of the foundational discoveries that underlay the biotechnology revolution, but then neglected to patent them. (This agreement was ultimately renegotiated after half a decade, after persistent complaints from other biotechnology firms, which argued that their inability to license public technologies was handicapping their progress.)

145

Yet despite its generous public backing and preferential access to technology, Celltech proved remarkably unsuccessful for much of its history. To be sure, the firm hired cutting-edge British academics and built modern laboratories, and entered into alliances with leading British firms. But after a decade, the firm's technologies were little closer to commercialization than on the day Celltech started. Outsider investors blamed a management team too focused on scientific research and a lack of accountability on the part of the government and related shareholders. Had an American venture-backed firm performed so poorly, they argued, it would have been shuttered long ago.

A new management team and a public offering put Celltech on a more stable course. Even here, though, the consequences for the British industry were mixed. One of the keystones of the firm's strategy was to exploit its access to the capital markets to acquire smaller British firms. While in some cases these deals led Celltech to products that it could develop and market, in many instances (such as Celltech's acquisition of RibosePharm and merger with Chiroscience) these transactions were counterproductive.[9] In some instances, the acquired company was spun out again in weaker shape a few years later; in other cases, progress in the development of the drugs of the acquired unit slowed or stopped.

Ultimately, Celltech was acquired in 2004 for a little over two billion dollars by a little-known Belgian drug company UCB (Union Chimique Belge). Many observers saw this ending as disappointing, For example, Aisling Burnand, chief executive of the UK Bioindustry Association noted, "One thing [the] Celltech [acquisition] definitely shows is that biotech company valuations are way too low, far below the real value in UK biotechnology." It is, of course, impossible to examine the parallel universe in which the British government decided not to pursue the Celltech initiative. But it is natural to wonder whether the preferential access to, and subsequent acquisitions of, promising entities by this troubled firm did not end up costing the British economy billions of pounds in lost economic opportunities.

A corollary to the necessary evaluation of potential recipients of funding is the need to evaluate public programs themselves on a periodic basis. These should be rigorous and dispassionate analyses of the programs' success to date. The evaluations should also consider the overall venture capital climate, and whether the economic rationales that justified the program's creation still apply.

The United States provides a clear example of the consequences of the failure to evaluate venture capital programs systematically. Many observers argue that the U.S. venture capital market is overfunded, and that the industry would have far higher returns if some of the more marginal groups were to exit the industry.[10] Certainly, the pool of venture funds today is many thousand times what it was when the SBIC program was established in 1958. Moreover, many of the participants in the SBIC program in the past two decades have been precisely these marginal firms, whose mandates do not differ appreciably from more established groups but are simply unable to raise capital from traditional sources owing to their shaky track records. Given these facts, it is proper to ask whether the program, however valuable in its initial manifestation, has outlived its usefulness. But the program has had no systematic evaluation over the years and remains politically popular.

Instead, lobbyists have repeatedly pushed Congress to hold hearings to consider a major expansion of the program. For instance, in the late 1990s, as the venture capital bubble was expanding, SBIC advocates made a major push to encourage the formation of a new quasi-public entity to be called the Venture Capital Marketing Association, or Vickie Mae. Modeled after the mortgage giant Fannie Mae (now, of course, a basket case), Vickie would have bought investments from SBICs that they could not take public or sell off to corporations. Instead, with an implicit government guarantee behind it, the new entity would sell bonds backed by these hard-to-sell firms (frequently called the "living dead" or "zombies" by venture capitalists). The arguments advanced by William Dunbar, at the time the head of Allied Investment Corporation, an SBIC, were representative of the arguments its advocates offered:

Creating Vickie Mae will allow the SBIC program, one of our country's most successful programs, to reach its full potential in helping America's entrepreneurs create the jobs and technologies that are the foundation of America's greatness.[11]

147

There was no effort in this testimony, or in other arguments by program advocates, to review the SBIC program's strengths and weaknesses, and determine whether the added subsidies were needed.

Fortunately for all of us, Congress—at the time controlled by free-market-leaning Republicans—did not buy the argument. One can only imagine how much worse the bubble years of 1999 and 2000 would have been had some of the most problematic venture firms been making investments secure in the knowledge that they could pass off onto a government-guaranteed corporation any firms that they could not take public. It's also likely that once the bubble burst, and Vickie Mae had to make good on its obligations, the value of these zombie firms would have shrunk dramatically, and the taxpayers would have been left making up the difference.

Of course, this systematic failure to undertake careful evaluations is not just an American or British phenomenon: it extends across the world. Over the course of the 1990s and first half of the next decade, for instance, various Chinese municipalities and provinces launched dozens of venture funds.[12] Many of them represented significant resources for the still-developing nation, such as the 650-million-renminbi fund launched by Jiangsu Province in 1992. But there was virtually no effort to evaluate the success of these early efforts, even if the initiatives faced incredible challenges: limited attractive investments, inexperienced deal teams, and the absence of many of the legal frameworks critical to making venture capital work. It is precisely at these times that assessing the consequences of venture efforts might be the most valuable.

The frequency of failure to evaluate makes the Israeli experience that much more striking. As we'll discuss later in this chapter, the Yozma program catalyzed the spectacular growth of entrepreneurship and venture capital in Israel. Nonetheless, after five years, the government examined the program and decided to auction off the ownership of Yozma.[13] This sale did not represent a shift of fashion, but rather was a planned step to be taken once the market had sufficiently matured. This ability to recognize when programs are no longer needed, and when scarce resources should be allocated elsewhere, is more the exception than the rule.

This brings us to a subtle problem: even if there are evaluations, they may look at the wrong things. In particular, far too often evaluations have relied on the compilation of success stories. Even organizations as august as the National Academy of Sciences have compiled assessments that consist of little more than anecdotes about firms that received government funding and then had commercial success.[14]

Not only can these misdirected evaluations lead to the wrong decisions about continuing programs, but they can result in programs that are less effective than if no evaluations had been done at all! How can this be? If the people evaluating programs are looking for success stories, the officials running the programs may select firms based on their likely success. In this case, they can claim credit for the happy endings. But this often translates into funding companies that don't need government funds. In the language of economics, the pressure of evaluation may drive program managers to fund companies for which the marginal contribution of public funds is very low.[15]

The Advanced Technology Program (ATP), whose failure to be flexible we discussed in the previous chapter, provides a cautionary tale in this regard.[16] The initial notion was to target generic, precompetitive technologies that the market had failed to fund. Thus, the idea was to create a diverse array of technologies in a variety of neglected fields.

Over time, however, the mission of the program mutated in an unpromising way. In the late 1990s, bureaucrats decided to target particular industries for focused grants. The industries they initially chose were Internet technologies and genomic sequencing. But these were not two randomly chosen sectors: at the time the program made its decision to proceed, they were flooded with money from investors. The promise of finding the "next Amazon.com" was leading everyone—from dentists to major corporations—to throw money at this sector. (The number of for-profit incubators catering to helping young Internet firms climbed from about 25 in 1997 to 320 in 2000.)[17] And the sequencing of the human genome had excited venture capitalists' imaginations about the possibility of curing long-standing diseases, leading to a smaller but still pronounced funding boom. While there were other sectors that held enormous technological promise and where entrepreneurs were struggling to raise money (alternative energy technologies, for one), these officials were drawn, like moths to a flame, to the sectors that were already overfunded by angel investors and venture funds alike.

It is hard not to attribute this decision to the questions about the ATP the Commerce Department was facing at the time from a skeptical, Republican-dominated Congress. The legislators had hard questions about whether the program was needed, and the program administrators were under tremendous pressure to demonstrate that the effort was a useful economic development tool. What better way to do so than to have a number of success stories to trot out, of companies that received ATP funding and then went public? And where to find companies likely to be successful than in the hottest area of the moment?

This decision may have been rational for the ATP bureaucrats eager to ensure their program's survival. But it was profoundly at odds with the program's mission to identify and rectify failures in the market for funding early-stage technologies. While an Internet firm that the program funded was perhaps more likely to go public and generate jobs than an obscure company working on advanced ceramics, the impact of the program's funds was much less in the online sector: in the late 1990s, everyone was trying to fund the next hot Internet idea. Even if the ATP had not given the online firm any funds, the start-up would still have been able to succeed. It was likely a very different story for the more neglected sectors.

If relying on success stories is not the best route to assess programs, how should these evaluations be done? In undertaking these assessments, one has to ask what would have happened without the subsidies. This may seem pretty daunting: we need to look inside a crystal ball, and figure out what would have happened in the parallel universe in which the program did not exist.

Ask ten economists how to overcome this research problem, and nine of them will give you the same one-word answer: randomization. This approach typically entails selecting some entities for awards that would not otherwise "make the cut," while not choosing some entities that would otherwise be chosen. The progress of these entities is then compared to their counterparts. The entrepreneurs who received awards that are below the cut-off score, and those who are above the line but did not get awards, are compared to their peers to get a sense of the program's impact.

The reason for this approach—which may seen as excessively complex and as introducing unnecessary complications—is a fear of unobserved differences. If these are not controlled for, the analysis may be flawed. To see how these considerations can affect conclusions, consider a dean of students, who is trying to persuade the admissions department to let in a hardworking student body. The dean is worried that certain student-athletes are excessively fun-loving: not only do they have poor grades, but their bad example deters their roommates from studying hard. The dean tests this idea by examining whether students who have athletes as roommates also seem to be having too much fun on campus—measured, for instance, by run-ins with the campus cops, or by being on academic probation. Indeed, he finds a relationship. The dean immediately fires off a memo to the college president, demanding that rugby and hockey players no longer be admitted because they are corrupting their fellow classmates.

The college president—trained as an economist—realizes there is a fundamental flaw with the dean's logic. Just because fun-loving students room together doesn't mean that the rugby players corrupt their roommates. Rather, it could be that fun-loving students chose to live together, or were placed together by administrators who didn't want to have to deal with disputes between incompatible roommates. To put it another way, just because the dean found an association between athletes and fun-loving roommates does not mean that the jocks are causing the problem.

The same worry appears when evaluating public programs to encourage entrepreneurship. Just because those entrepreneurs who take part in a government program do better than their peers doesn't mean the program has made a difference. Rather, the applicants could have been disproportionately the best and the brightest entrepreneurs, who were smart enough to learn about the program and find the time to fill out the application. Moreover, if there was a competition for the rewards, the screening process should have picked out the better groups. Thus, the awardees are not randomly chosen.

The reader might object that there are easier ways to solve this research problem. One idea might be to control for the characteristics of the awardees. This idea is behind a number of the analyses described in this volume, where a researcher matched awardees with, for instance, other firms in the same industry of about the same size. But we still might worry that there are differences in other, unobserved characteristics of the companies that we're not able to see or control for, and which may affect our conclusions dramatically. By randomly selecting which entrepreneurs receive awards and which don't, these worries are greatly reduced.

Another objection to randomization is that it's wrong to knowingly give public money to an inferior entrepreneur. While we have long been comfortable with the use of randomized trials in medical research, where one set of cancer patients gets the experimental drug and the others get the traditional treatment, the introduction of random choices in economic development settings make many leaders profoundly nervous. Whatever the merits of their reluctance, it has blocked attempts to use randomization while assessing public venturing programs.

Fortunately, there is an alternative: the use of an approach called "regression discontinuity" analyses. Essentially, this type of analysis exploits the fact that when program managers do their assessment of potential participants, there are always going to be some applications that fall just above or just below the cut-off line. By comparing these entrepreneurs or venture funds, which are likely to be very similar to each other in everything except for the fact that some were chosen for the program and others not, one can get a good sense of the program's impact without a randomization procedure. As Adam Jaffe, one of the most vocal advocates of better evaluation approaches, has observed:

> I and others have previously harped on randomization as the "gold standard" for program evaluation. I now believe that [regression discontinuity] design represents a better trade-off between statistical benefits and resistance to implementation.[18]

152

Importance of a Global Perspective

The final lesson regarding implementation is that governments should emphasize the development of strong interconnections with venture funds elsewhere. Venture capital is an increasingly global business, where strong connections to major markets seem critical to success. Growing a venture capital industry in isolation, however appealing to policymakers, is unlikely to be a winning strategy.

A dramatic example of this globalization is Skype.[19] When it received its initial venture financing in 2003, Skype was the very definition of a company in "stealth mode." In 2000, Skype's eventual founders, Niklas Zennstrom and Janus Friis, invented a program called Kazaa. It enabled users to readily download music and video content from other users' computers. Such a peer-to-peer sharing system may sound innocent enough, but rights to the vast majority of the material traded on the Kazaa network weren't owned by the people doing the trading: the material was movies and music copyrighted by major studios and production companies, which did not take kindly to the loss of revenues they attributed to Kazaa.

By late 2003, with more than 300 million copies of Kazaa downloaded—the most of any program in the world—Zennstrom and Friis had emerged as two of the chief enemies of the music business. It was questionable whether Kazaa actually violated copyright law as it stood at the time: the program essentially served as a platform for traders, rather than directly being involved in trades. Furthermore, the two founders had severed most of their ties with the company. But despite these considerations, the pair were being pursued by music firms, their lawyers, and henchmen. As a result, the company was extremely secretive, not revealing the location of its Europe-based offices and the identities of the Estonian programmers who made up the heart of the firm.

While Skype used the same peer-to-peer technology as Kazaa, it was for a very different application: it offered the ability to call peers essentially for free over the Internet. As long as both callers have microphones and the Skype software, they can readily talk to each other. Once again, the users' own computers—rather than some network that the firm built—did the hard work of finding the other party, converting the sounds into digital signals, directing them onward. At the time, the firm estimated that it cost Vonage, the leading provider of Internet telephony using a traditional centralized model, $400 to add a customer. A new customer for Skype, by way of contrast, cost one-tenth of a cent.

This value proposition was enough to attract some of the leading venture investors, despite the far-flung and secretive nature of the firm. Bessemer Venture Partners, Draper Fisher Jurvetson, and Index Ventures, among others, led an initial financing round of a few million dollars; larger financings soon followed. Despite the fact that Skype's far-flung and rapidly changing group resisted close supervision—and that the venture groups had little ability to provide oversight "on the ground" to programmers in Estonia—the investors were willing to bet that the experience of the management team would lead to a successful firm. And indeed their confidence was justified: eBay bought the firm in 2005 for $2.6 billion, giving the "A" round investors more than a hundred-fold return.

The increased globalization of the venture capital industry can be seen along three dimensions:

- The first is in capital commitments by limited partners. Venture capital markets used to be extremely segmented: German limited partners invested in Germany, French investors in France, and so forth. Over time, however, these barriers have broken down, and international capital flows have become far more common. For instance, in Europe, in 1993, only 19 percent of funds raised by venture and buyout groups were from capital sources based outside of Europe. By 2007, the percentage was up to 34 percent. In the most successful markets, such as Great Britain, the domestic shares are even lower: only one-quarter of the capital is from sources within the United Kingdom.[20]

- The second dimension is the changing location of investments by venture capitalists. In previous years, many venture groups emphasized the importance of investing extremely locally, often

154

within an hour's drive of the office. Over time, however, long-distance investing has become far more commonplace. The explosive growth of opportunities in India and China, coupled with successful deals elsewhere, has opened individuals' eyes to the potential of long-distance investing.

- The final, and perhaps most critical, dimension is in the deployment of resources by entrepreneurial firms themselves. In the past few years, it has become commonplace for even the youngest Silicon Valley firm to have an overseas presence. Typically, these groups will employ programmers in India (if a software concern) or design and production experts in China (if a firm selling hardware) almost as soon as they are formed. These extensions allow the entrepreneurs to produce far more output from each dollar invested than they would had they confined their hiring to domestic markets. Moreover, doing work abroad allows the firms to get their products to the market more quickly. As a result, venture capitalists are spending far more time in Asia supervising the far-flung operations of their portfolio firms, or even opening offices in these nations.

In some cases, these global connections can arrive without government intervention. Eastern Canada in recent years offers an example. The venture capital industry has expanded, largely because of its close ties to the United States. First, local transactions have appeared increasingly attractive to funds based in Boston and New York: the disparity in valuations between eastern Canada and the United States has meant that stakes in comparable companies have been available at a substantial discount. Second, Ontario- and Quebec-based funds are increasingly attracting limited partners based in the United States as investors in their new funds.

But unless a nation is lucky enough to be proximate to a venture hub, effective government policy is likely to be helpful in catalyzing the globalization process. This point can be illustrated by comparing two case studies: the experiences in Israel and Japan.[21]

In June 1992, the Israeli government established Yozma Venture

155

Capital Ltd., a $100 million fund wholly owned by the public sector. At the time, there was a single venture fund active in the nation, Athena Venture Partners. While there were certainly well-trained engineers in the nation working on promising technologies, entrepreneurs (and would-be company founders) were suspicious of venture investors. This reluctance was based in part on their interactions with the pioneering venture capitalists in the nation, as well as their general skepticism about selling equity to unaffiliated parties. Instead, they preferred to rely on bank debt for financing. The only problem, of course, was that such financing was rarely available for young, risky ventures.

The key goal of Yozma was to bring foreign venture capitalists' investment expertise and network of contacts to Israel. The need for this assistance was highlighted by the failure of the nation's earlier efforts to promote high-technology entrepreneurship. One assessment concluded that fully 60 percent of the entrepreneurs in prior programs had been successful in meeting their technical goals but nonetheless failed because the entrepreneurs were unable to market their products or raise capital for further development.[22] Foreign expertise was seen as key to overcoming this problem.

Accordingly, Yozma actively discouraged Israeli financiers from participating in its programs. Rather, the focus was on getting foreign venture investors to commit capital for Israeli entrepreneurs. The government provided matching funds to investors, typically $8 million of a $20 million fund. The venture fund was given the right to buy back the government stake within the first five years for the initial value plus a preset interest rate of roughly 5 to 7 percent. Thus, the incentives of Yozma meant that the government provided an added incentive to the venture fund if the investments proved successful. Moreover, learning from the nation's misadventures during earlier programs to stimulate the venture industry—when cumbersome application procedures and burdensome reporting requirements discouraged participation—the administration of the program was deliberately made simple.

In addition to the financial incentives, the project adopted a legal structure for the venture funds that foreign investors would be comfortable with. Included were features such as a ten-year fund life, limited partnerships modeled after the Delaware partnerships that are standard practices in the United States and elsewhere, and "flow through" tax status. Had the government not adopted these features—and the Israeli Treasury department resisted them before acquiescing under pressure—it is unlikely that the program would have succeeded in attracting foreign investors.

The Yozma program delivered beyond the wildest dreams of the founders. Ten groups took advantage of this offer, mostly from the United States, Western Europe, and Japan. Many of the original Yozma funds, including Gemini and Walden Ventures, earned spectacular returns and served as precursors to larger, follow-on funds. Moreover, many of the local partners recruited by the overseas venture capitalists were able to spin off and establish their own firms, which global investors were eager to fund because of their impressive track records. (A Yozma "alumni club" allows groups to learn from each others' experiences while making these transitions.) One decade after the program's inception, the ten original Yozma groups were managing Israeli funds totaling $2.9 billion, and the Israeli venture market had expanded to include 60 groups managing approximately $10 billion.[23] The magnitude of this success is also suggested in figure 6.1, which shows that the ratio of venture investment to GDP is far higher in Israel than elsewhere. In most tabulations, Tel Aviv has surpassed Boston as the urban area with the most venture activity after San Francisco.

Japan is a study in contrast. It has also provided direct financial assistance to entrepreneurial firms, but with a very localized focus.[24] Both the Ministry of International Trade and Industry and Japan Development Bank (JDB) developed programs that offer financial assistance to young, entrepreneurial firms. This assistance has taken a variety of forms, from actual operating facilities ("incubators") to equity investments and loans. For instance, JDB established a fund to provide five-year loans at subsidized rates (typically 3.25 percent and less) to young high-tech firms—loans that the bank secured through these firms' patents and other intellectual property. And in late 1996, JDB

raised capital from more than a hundred corporations and government agencies to make traditional equity investments.

But throughout, there was no effort to encourage the involvement of
foreign venture capitalists or others. In fact, the investments were typically structured in ways that were quite alien to outsiders. These efforts
were almost uniformly unsuccessful, and venture capital activity in
Japan has plummeted in recent years. In large part, this decline reflects the lack of fresh perspectives: given the strength of technological
innovation in Japanese firms and the depth of many academic departments in its universities, it is hard to believe that there are not innovations waiting to be commercialized. But the domestic venture industry
was never particularly strong at screening, adding value, and monitoring entrepreneurs: instead, it was a very bureaucratic process that was
largely in the hands of bank and insurance company affiliates. The incentives introduced by the various government programs were not designed to attract overseas groups with the key skill sets, and these
groups have continued to largely ignore the market.

The benefits of global connections are manifold. But within the political process, the imperatives of satisfying domestic audiences can
lead to distortions. When Australia legalized the venture capital limited partnership structure in 2002, for instance, legislators worried that
foreign funds or firms might exploit the favorable tax treatment these
entities enjoyed.[25] So they required that each company backed by a
venture partnership have at least half its assets in Australia. The pioneering funds found the companies in their portfolio handicapped, as
the entrepreneurs could not expand their software development activities in India or their manufacturing operations in China without putting the venture funds' tax status in danger.

Local venture capital industries can benefit enormously from being
well connected to the global market. Such connections are likely to
lead to knowledge flows to local venture capitalists, follow-on capital
to portfolio firms, and an ability to raise larger follow-on funds. The
changing nature of the venture capital process implies that these ties
are more readily established than in years past. Meanwhile, to build
a venture capital industry in isolation is a recipe for irrelevance and
failure.

Putting It All Together

So far, we have looked at the various elements that government can use to boost entrepreneurial activity—for instance, tax policies, boosts to technology transfer, and subsidies to entrepreneurs—in isolation. Ideally, of course, these elements should be viewed collectively. Are there certain steps that work well together? Are there other combinations that should be avoided?

Here, alas, we must reemphasize the early state of our knowledge. While it is undoubtedly important to understand how the pieces of government policy fit together, we're still not in a position to say much definitive about their interrelationships.

We can illustrate this point by considering one of the most ambitious research efforts to fit the pieces together, an essay by Christian Keuschnigg.[26] He considers a setting where governments can use a variety of weapons:

- Subsidies for investments for venture capitalists

- Subsidies or taxes on sales or profits of large or start-up firms

- Funding of basic research

Practical-minded readers may object that this list leaves out many other strategies that we have discussed. But, as we'll soon see, an analysis of even this limited number of options proves troublingly difficult.

Keuschnigg points out that policymakers need to be simultaneously active on several fronts. Otherwise, distortions may creep in that leave entrepreneurs worse off than before. For instance, what happens if the government just subsidizes start-ups (for instance, through tax credits)? We might assume that this subsidy will increase the profits of entrepreneurs and venture capitalists. But it may lure more entrepreneurs and venture capitalists into the market, so that, unless the supply of good ideas grows, more firms and financiers are chasing after the same ideas. This competition may depress returns, and ultimately discourage entrepreneurs and venture investors. What seems like a reasonable policy turns out to be self-defeating.

159

So far, so good. We see that policymakers need to identify the right combination of actions to achieve the optimal effects. But it is at this point that things get complicated. In particular, after running various optimization analyses, Keuschnigg suggests that many of the classic remedies—like supporting research or subsidizing venture capital investments—are not ideal. Rather, to boost entrepreneurship, policymakers should be subsidizing *mature* firms, perhaps even with some penalties for start-ups! His intuition is that by making the fruits of success really sweet, entrepreneurs will work even harder (and venture capitalists be even more willing to fund them), without the distortions that his model suggests are the by-product of subsidizing start-ups.

The basic idea behind Keuschnigg's analysis—that piecemeal policies aimed at helping entrepreneurs may have harmful consequences—appears to be reasonable. But it is hard to know how many of his rather puzzling results are a function of the model itself. To arrive at these results, the analysis has to make several assumptions that seem contrary to the behavior of real officials and real entrepreneurs:

- The model requires policymakers to have a lot of information about the production costs, preferences, and innovative potential of the various players in the economy. As we have seen, in many instances, government officials in fact have very little information about the basic actors and their incentives, much less the specific industries they are targeting.

- The government in the model must be able to implement a complex system and subsidies. In actuality, even if government officials want to implement the socially ideal system (and this is a big if!), we know that individuals and firms have boundless creativity when it comes to avoiding taxes and maximizing subsidies.

- While government officials have a great deal of flexibility in developing and implementing complex programs, the model strictly limits the ability of entrepreneurs and venture investors to solve their various problems by entering into complex and creative contracts, as they frequently do in real life.

Thus, Keuschnigg's model illustrates how far economists need to go in thinking about policy packages, and the challenges researchers face before they will be able to answer the questions that policymakers struggle with. We economists have a way to go before we can present our own "unified field theory" of how government can help entrepreneurs.

FINAL THOUGHTS

The effective implementation of public venturing programs may initially seem a dry and esoteric topic. But as the many examples discussed in this chapter have suggested, effective implementation is vitally important. To successfully promote entrepreneurship and venture capital, public officials must correctly make many choices.

In this chapter, we've highlighted three areas where efforts have often gone astray. The design of effective incentive schemes helps ensure that the players receiving the subsidies, whether entrepreneurs or venture capitalists, only benefit at the same time as society as a whole and limits opportunistic self-dealing. Rigorous evaluations can ensure that the right people are attracted to government programs, and that the initiatives themselves are well designed. And a strong international orientation can maximize the chance that best practices are effectively absorbed.

In the next chapter, we'll turn to a special sort of public venture capital, the sovereign wealth fund. These government investment pools face many of the same issues that the programs we have discussed in this book have grappled with, but their size and visibility introduces additional issues.

CHAPTER 8

THE SPECIAL CHALLENGES OF SOVEREIGN FUNDS

Perhaps the most dramatic setting where governments have struggled with the challenges of being venture capitalists has been sovereign wealth funds. These funds, owned by a state that invests in various financial assets, represent in some sense the ultimate challenge in governmental support of entrepreneurship. In addition to the obstacles that all public efforts to boost entrepreneurship face, the size, demands for visibility, and complex mission of sovereign wealth funds are daunting.

This chapter will review the many issues these new investors encounter. After an overview of these complex institutions, we'll discuss both the similarities to other public venture programs and the additional challenges sovereign funds face.

We will then consider how they can operate effectively. There appears to be no good answer to one critical question, how to cope with demands for transparency. Interests in many Western nations demand that sovereign funds provide detailed accountings of their activities. This request for openness can be readily understood, but such disclosures are likely to make it harder for sovereign funds to achieve their goals.

The available evidence offers more clear-cut advice when it comes to the challenges associated with the large size of sovereign funds. A number of approaches cultivated by effective institutional investors worldwide—from investing in the best people to pioneering new asset classes to compartmentalizing investment activities—seem readily applicable to these investors.

An Overview of Sovereign Wealth Funds

Depending on how one counts, there are between forty and seventy different sovereign funds, run by political entities as disparate as New Mexico and Kazakhstan. (Tables 8.1 and 8.2 illustrate the largest sovereign wealth funds and estimates of their holdings and growth.)[1] Market estimates of their size are difficult to determine because they often lack transparency: disclosure regulations and practices differ widely from country to country. But in mid-2008, J.P. Morgan estimated that total fund assets were nearly $3.5 trillion.[2] To place this figure in a broad investment context: the amount these funds currently manage exceeds the $1.4 trillion managed by hedge funds, but it is only 1.2 percent of global financial assets, which are about $190 trillion.

The wealth of sovereign funds has differing origins. In many of the most visible cases, such as Abu Dhabi, petroleum has been the source of abundant wealth. Other commodities, from diamonds to phos-

Table 8-1
Sovereign Funds with Over $100 Billion in Assets in Mid-2008

Country	Fund Name	Year of Inception	Estimated Assets Under Management in Mid-2008 ($ billions)
United Arab Emirates	Abu Dhabi Investment Authority	1976	875
Norway	Government Pension Fund	1990	390
Singapore	Government Investment Corporation	1981	330
Saudi Arabia	Saudi Arabia Monetary Authority	1952	327
Kuwait	Kuwait Investment Authority	1982	250
China	China Investment Corporation	2007	200
Hong Kong	Hong Kong Monetary Authority	1998	186
Russia	Oil and Gas Fund	2004	128
Singapore	Temasek Holding	1974	115

163

Table 8-2
Projected Sovereign Wealth Fund Growth

	Low commodity price / return scenario	High commodity price / return scenario
Assets under management at year-end 2007 ($ trillions)	3.0	3.0
Assets under management at year-end 2012 ($ trillions)	5.0	9.3
Annual growth rate in assets	10.8%	25.4%

phates, have been the foundation of other funds. Still others have been primarily funded from the proceeds from privatizations, that is, the sale of state-owned properties or businesses. Many other funds, such as those of China and Singapore, have their origin in trade surpluses.

Most of their growth has occurred recently. In 1990, for example, fund assets were estimated at only $500 billion. Over the past three years, they have achieved a 24 percent annual growth rate and could grow to $12 trillion of assets—a growth rate of $1 trillion a year—over the next eight years.[3] Much of this growth has been driven, not surprisingly, by the rising price of petroleum, and has been concentrated in producer nations such as Norway, the United Arab Emirates, and Kuwait. But other important players include nations such as China that pile up foreign currency because they run persistent, large trade surpluses. These countries less and less often put these reserves "under a mattress"—that is, holding safe but low-return Treasury bonds—and are instead seeking broader portfolios.

Sovereign funds frequently have multiple goals, which different organizations emphasize to varying extents. The most powerful motivation can be seen in the experience of Kiribati, a collection of islands in the Pacific Ocean formerly known as the Gilbert Islands, with a population of under 100,000 residents.[4] For many decades, the dominant export from the country was guano, bird droppings used for fertilizer. The island's leaders set up the Kiribati Revenue Equalization Reserve Fund in 1956, and imposed a tax on production by foreign firms. The last guano was extracted in 1979, but the fund remains a key economic contributor. At $600 million, it is ten times the size of the nation's gross domestic product, and the interest generated by the fund represents 30 percent of the nation's revenue.

There are three distinct roles sovereign wealth funds can play:

- They can serve as a source of capital for future generations, who will no longer be able to rely on commodities for a steady stream of revenue. Such a use is similar to that of a university that receives a major bequest: typically, these funds are not spent immediately, but instead added to its endowment so it can benefit many cohorts of students.

- They can play the role of smoothing revenues. Countries that depend on commodities for the bulk of their exports can be whipsawed by shifts in prices, as, for instance, many oil exporters were in the mid-1980s and late 1990s.

- Finally, these funds can serve as holding companies, in which the government places its strategic investments. Public leaders may see fit to invest in domestic or foreign firms for strategic purposes, and the sovereign funds provide a way to hold and manage these stakes.

THE GRIM LEGACY

In attempting to save money for the future, nations are departing from a long legacy of failure in managing the wealth created by natural resources. Consider, for instance, the experience of Norway in the 1970s and 1980s.[5] In the oil surge of those years, the government received a tremendous windfall of funds from its numerous rigs in the North Sea. While efforts were made to enact legislation that set aside money for the future, no savings were made. Instead, the money was largely spent immediately.

Some of the spending benefited physical and social infrastructure: Norway rebuilt its excellent system of roads and bridges and provided free health care and higher education to all residents. But other expenditures were less beneficial. Minimum wages were set extremely

165

high, several times the level in the United States. While well intentioned, this step rendered a number of economic sectors uncompetitive. Much of the funding for industry was earmarked for dying sectors, such as shipbuilding. This support allowed facilities to remain open for a few years more, but could not reverse the industries' inexorable decline. Much of the funding for new ventures went to friends or relatives of parliamentarians or of the bureaucrats responsible for allocating the funds.

Moreover, the policy of aggressively spending the government's petroleum revenues introduced chaos into public and private finances when the oil price plunged in the mid-1980s. The government's oil revenue dropped from about $11.2 billion in 1985—or about 20 percent of Norway's gross domestic product—to $2.4 billion in 1988. The resulting retrenchment of public spending and tightening of credit led numerous banks to fail. The resulting downturn also led to an unprecedented wave of bankruptcies by private citizens.

Nor was Norway the first nation to struggle with the influx of wealth, or what the *Economist* has termed the "Dutch Disease" (named after the economic malaise that gripped the Netherlands when it experienced an influx of natural gas royalties during the 1960s). Turning much further back in time, the historian David Landes documents the corrosive effects that the tremendous wealth generated by Spain's overseas conquests had on the nation's economy. Consider a communication from the Moroccan ambassador to Spain in 1690:

> The Spanish nation today possesses the greatest wealth and the largest income of all the Christians. But the love of luxury and the comforts of civilization have overcome them, and you will rarely find one of this nation who engages in trade or travels abroad for commerce as do the other Christian nations. . . . Most of those who practice [handi]crafts in Spain are Frenchmen [who] flock to Spain to look for work . . . [and] in a short time make great fortunes.[6]

The "curse of natural resources" is a well-established pattern. In his exercise to determine the impact of different variables on economic growth, titled "I Just Ran Two Million Regressions," Xavier Sala-i-Martin seeks to explain growth rates across a large number of nations between 1960 and 1995.[7] He finds that roughly ten sets of variables have consistent explanatory power, including geography (being farther away from the equator is better for growth), the economic system (capitalist societies grow more quickly), and religion (Buddhist, Confucian, and Muslim nations experienced faster growth than Catholic and Protestant ones). Among these consistent variables is the abundance of natural resources—measured using the share of exports from agricultural and extractive industries—which has a negative impact on growth. This finding has been echoed in many papers.

But where does this curse come from?[8] One suggestion is that it may reflect a crowding-out effect. Nations that devote more of their resources—for instance, public spending and management talent—to exploiting oil and other commodities weaken their manufacturing and services sectors. For instance, manufacturers may struggle to find talented people at reasonable wages, and may find it hard to export because the nation's currency is strong relative to others. And it may be that a healthy manufacturing and service sector is critical to long-run growth.

Another possibility is that an abundance of natural resources exacerbates the capture problems we discussed in chapter 4. The profits from natural resource projects are typically concentrated in a few, easily identified hands. The temptation for government officials to guide benefits to their friends (and sometimes themselves), rather than choose policies that would be best for the nation's future growth, may become too large. Moreover, the easy profits from such shakedowns may lure the most talented people into unproductive—though very lucrative—jobs in the public sector, when society as a whole would be much better off if they pursued entrepreneurial efforts. These dynamics might lead natural-resource-dependent countries to have poorer governments, less innovation, and ultimately lower growth. Even if public corruption is not widespread, active public management of the natural resources can lead to an economy where the public and private sectors are intertwined. While there are exceptions, often these intermeshed economies are less flexible than their alternatives.

167

Sovereign funds can address these downsides of a wealth of natural resources—and potentially undo the negative relationship between growth and natural resources—in two ways. First, by not spending the gains from natural resources immediately, but rather preserving them for future generations, the distorting impact of the windfall is reduced. Had the Norwegian government kept public spending in check during the 1970s and 1980s, it is unlikely that the disruptions in subsequent years would have been as severe. Second, earmarking a percentage of natural resources revenues into an investment fund may reduce capture problems. Such a step reduces the likelihood that government officials will spend these revenues in an unwise or corrupt manner—assuming, that is, the sovereign fund is run in a professional manner.

THE FUTURE OF SOVEREIGN FUNDS

In some ways, then, these are the best of times for sovereign funds: they have experienced tremendous growth and are likely to continue to do so. In a number of cases, the size and sophistication of the investment teams employed have grown substantially. A number of these groups have abandoned overly conservative strategies and adopted allocations more consistent with "best practices": for instance, Norway's Government Pension Fund increased its allocation to emerging markets and real estate in May 2008.

But at the same time, sovereign wealth funds face a raft of challenges. Many of them are common to other government venture promotion schemes more generally: for instance, the temptation to invest too locally without considering broader options, a failure to assess performance, and pressures to invest in the "pet projects" of political leaders and their associates. But they also face two additional pressures, which make leading such an organization particularly challenging.

Challenge 1: Visibility
The first of these is the increased political scrutiny of these organizations in many nations. Although sovereign wealth funds have existed for more than five decades, they have attracted considerable attention

168

recently because of their accelerating growth and because of highly public transactions that drew them into the global spotlight, such as the $7.5 billion investment in Citigroup in November 2007 by the Abu Dhabi Investment Authority. The controversies surrounding investments by sovereign funds are not new—witness the 1987 row over the Kuwait Investment Office's purchase of a 20 percent stake in British Petroleum—yet the intensity of scrutiny in recent years has been unprecedented. Nor is it likely to subside, at least if the growth of these funds continues unabated.

What is behind this fear of sovereign funds? In part, it can be attributed to intense anxiety in many established economies about globalization and the changing global balance of power. It is far easier to blame an institution than vaguely understood economic forces.

Indeed, many of the fears about sovereign funds appear misplaced. Press accounts and political rhetoric have depicted these funds as focusing their investments on politically sensitive sectors in the most developed nations, and suggested that they pose a strategic risk to these nations. For instance, former U.S. Treasury secretary and Harvard president Larry Summers has stated,

> The logic of the capitalist system depends on shareholders causing companies to act so as to maximize the value of their shares. It is far from obvious that this will over time be the only motivation of governments as shareholders. They may want to see their national companies compete effectively, or to extract technology or to achieve influence.[9]

Whatever the reasonableness of Summers's critique on a theoretical level, it does not seem to describe real-world behaviors. A recent Monitor Group study showed that the bulk of investments focused on domestic and emerging markets, rather than the West. If anything, these investors have tended to shy away from high-profile sectors in developed nations: the investments in 2007 and 2008 in ailing financial services firms (particularly investment banks) were the exception rather than the rule.[10] (Based on the miserable subsequent performance of many of these financial firms, many funds probably wish they had not taken this detour.) And it is hard to deny that these investments during the credit crunch were beneficial to the United States and other developed countries, as they introduced much-needed liquidity into the financial system at a critical time.

But at the same time, the sovereign funds have not helped themselves with the intense secrecy that surrounds some of their activities. Greater visibility—publicizing the size of the pools, investment strategies, and particular investments—could help dispel at least part of the worries over sovereign funds.

Valuable lessons may be drawn from the experiences of the private equity industry. Buyout funds have operated happily in the shadows for many decades. In recent years, however, they have been singled out for scrutiny in many Western nations. To cite just a few examples:

- Franz Müntefering, the head of the Social Democratic Party (and subsequently the vice-chancellor of Germany), attacked private equity groups and hedge funds, describing them as "swarms of locusts that fall on companies, stripping them bare before moving on."[11] A leaked party document listed a number of such "locusts," including the Carlyle Group and Goldman Sachs.

- Korean authorities, angered at the profits that Carlyle, Newbridge Capital, and Lone Star have made from their investments there, have launched enforcement actions, including raids on the offices of private equity groups.

- In both Japan and China, the government has proposed new rules affecting the taxation and regulation of activities of foreign investment funds. At least in part, these actions have been triggered by anger over the success of groups such as Ripplewood.

- A number of European nations have changed the tax treatment of private equity, such as Denmark's imposition of limitations on the deductibility of interest payments.

Many of the charges leveled against the private equity industry—such as claims that buyouts are typically associated with massive job losses or short-term horizons—do not stand up to scrutiny. For instance, while private equity investments in the United States do seem to be associated with slower job growth (or faster job losses) than at comparable firms, this effect is almost entirely offset by the greater level of job creation at new facilities by bought-out firms. Looking at one particular form of long-run investment, the pursuit of innovation, also paints a very different picture than that depicted by the critics. Rather than cutting back on innovation, the aggregate level stays roughly the same after a buyout. But the awards applied for by private equity-backed firms prove to be far more economically impactful than the ones sought earlier. In short, the firms seem to rearrange their research portfolios, substituting high-impact efforts for the more marginal activities pursued before the buyout.[12] While there is certainly behavior by buyout firms to criticize—in particular, the periodic periods of overheating that characterize the industry, when too cheap debt leads to a flurry of excessive leverage and overpriced transactions—many of the claims by the industry's critics seem overstated.

Despite the dubious foundation of many critiques, they have attracted attention from the media, politicians, and voters alike. As I discussed above, these charges have affected public policymaking in important ways. Leaders' concerns about economic disruption and the secrecy of the industry seem to have exacerbated this reaction.

It is important for sovereign funds, like the private equity industry, to address these concerns proactively. Ensuring transparency about the story behind the funds, the way they operate, and the consequences of investments is important. Encouraging objective research by outsiders that can better document the funds' roles and performance can also help alleviate doubts.

At the same time, two cautions should be noted. First, too much disclosure can have real costs. The costs can be seen most dramatically on American college campuses. In recent years, student activists at a number of elite universities have demanded greater disclosure of their endowment's holdings. Yet, the endowment managers have vigorously resisted these cries.

Does the endowment chieftains' reluctance to provide detailed information about their holdings mean they have something to hide? Why else would they be unwilling to reveal what they own? In truth, there are reasons to maintain some secrecy.

A crucial issue is that the strategies of the elite investors—whether endowments, pensions, or sovereign wealth funds—are being scrutinized and imitated as never before. In the past, there was often a substantial lag between the time endowments first began investing in an asset class and the time other institutions followed. For instance, many of the Ivy League schools began investing in venture capital in the early 1970s, but most corporate and public pensions did not follow until the 1980s and 1990s, respectively. But today, the lags are much shorter. Within a couple of years of Harvard's initiating a program to invest in forestland, for instance, many other institutions had adopted similar initiatives. The same dynamics also play themselves out at the individual fund level: an investment by an elite endowment into a fund can trigger a rush of capital seeking to gain access to the same fund. Such an influx can make it much harder for the investor to continue its successful strategy. Thus, the greater disclosure demanded by campus protestors would likely intensify the problem of imitative investment, leading to lower returns and fewer resources for future generations of students. Detailed disclosures by sovereign funds could lead to the same problems.

Furthermore, even an aggressive policy of encouraging transparency will not solve all of the challenges that sovereign wealth funds face. Investment decisions that would seem unremarkable when made by an individual or institutional investor can become political hot potatoes when undertaken by a sovereign fund. Consider, for instance, the experience of Norway's Government Pension Fund.[13] When the fund trimmed its portfolio of firms using child labor, it sold $400 million of Wal-Mart stock. This decision triggered a diplomatic row with the American ambassador, who accused Norway of passing "essentially a national judgment on the ethics of the [company]." (The fund pointed out that when it had shared with Wal-Mart its draft report presenting evidence about the company's labor practices, Wal-Mart ignored it.) Similarly, when the Norway's fund, along with many hedge funds, presciently sold short the shares of Icelandic banks in 2006, it triggered a major diplomatic row with that nation.

Challenge 2: Maintaining Returns

The second challenge sovereign wealth funds must address is that of ensuring attractive investment returns. Strategies that work for a modest-sized institution—for instance, a university endowment with a few billion dollars under management—may be difficult to scale up into a larger organization. For instance, it may be possible for a billion-dollar endowment to generate attractive returns from investments of $10 million apiece in equities in second-tier exchanges and in developing markets. If a sovereign fund with 100 times the capital were to pursue a similar strategy, it would probably (*a*) be unable to identify enough attractive investments to have a return that significantly boosts that of the overall fund; or (*b*) find that purchases of larger blocks of stock so affected the market price that the strategy was far less profitable. Indeed, many endowments have struggled to maintain their success as they have become larger. Thus, for the larger sovereign funds, generating attractive returns is by no means simple.

This problem is particularly acute as sovereign funds put more emphasis on alternative investments, such as private equity and real estate. These sectors have been critical to the extraordinary success university endowments have enjoyed. For instance, when one examines the investment performance of Ivy League schools between 2002 and 2005, the only word that can characterize it is "spectacular": funds earned almost 12 percent annually in a period when most market indexes did far worse. This result is inexorably linked to the funds' use of alternative investments: when one compares the funds' earnings during these years to benchmarks, fully 94 percent of the excess performance can be attributed to hedge funds, private equity, real estate, and venture capital.[14]

But academic research suggests that these sectors are particularly vulnerable to influxes of new capital. Because there are often limited opportunities in a given sector, additional capital tends to be associated with unfortunate events, as we saw during the "venture bubble" of

173

the late 1990s and the "buyout bubble" of 2005–7. These periods typically see the entry of many new funds, which tend to perform much more poorly than established groups. Groups already in the market raise larger funds: rapid growth, while it leads to more fees for the fund managers, is also associated with a decline in returns. Even groups that remain disciplined and resist the temptation to grow may find their returns suffering in a more competitive market. In many instances, the phenomenon of "money chasing deals" leads all firms to pay higher prices to acquire firms than in normal times. In venture capital, for instance, a doubling of flows of funds into the sector is associated with funds paying between 7 and 21 percent more for an otherwise identical transaction.[15] All these factors—the entry of inexperienced investors, too rapid growth among established players, and the purchase of securities at higher prices—lead to lower returns. Because some sovereign funds are so large, there is a good probability that their moves into alternatives will coincide with periods of overinvestment.

Moreover, the various goals that motivate sovereign funds may be in conflict. Given the relative youth of most sovereign funds, this conflict is difficult to illustrate, but we can look at the experiences of other long-term investors. A stark example is the University of Rochester, which in the early 1970s had the third largest endowment in the country (after Harvard and the University of Texas).[16] The administrators responsible for it made the fateful choice to heavily allocate investments to local companies such as Kodak and Xerox, which suffered substantial reverses during the 1970s and 1980s. As a result of this miscue and others, Rochester suffered poor returns in these decades. By 1995, its endowment was only the twenty-fifth largest in the nation. As a result of financial troubles largely brought about by its underperforming endowment, it was forced to dramatically downsize its faculty and programs in the mid-1990s. In this case, the goal of supporting local businesses ran counter to the goal of buffering the university against financial shortfalls.

Thus, sovereign funds have to figure out how to grow rapidly while generating attractive investment returns. The task is not an easy one. But three approaches across the world of institutional investors stand out as models, which are well worth serious consideration.

Be independent minded. First, it does not make sense to emulate exactly the allocations and approaches that have been successful for others in the past. Markets that generated extraordinary returns in earlier years are unlikely to continue to do so. For instance, endowments such as Harvard's and Yale's have benefited tremendously from Silicon Valley–based venture capital funds over the past three-and-a-half decades.

But for a sovereign wealth fund beginning an alternative investment program today, this route is unlikely to be lucrative. It is virtually impossible for a new investor to get access to the top-tier U.S.-based venture groups, who have generated most of the outsized returns in the sector. Moreover, because the sector has matured, returns will likely be far more modest than in the 1980s and 1990s.

Instead, relatively undiscovered investment classes seem like a far more rewarding strategy. Whether African stocks or infrastructure projects in central Asia, these new classes of investments are similar to the pioneering Silicon Valley venture funds in the early 1970s. To be sure, there are enormous risks, and even the range of possible outcomes is not fully understood. But if the apparent opportunities in these sectors materialize, and the sovereign funds can find the right teams to work with, these new areas are likely to yield attractive returns to the funds for many years to come.

Invest in the best people. Second, building a successful program is a major investment. Without a long-run investment strategy and a process of careful evaluation and strategic fine-tuning, returns are likely to be poor. Both of these factors depend critically on the recruitment and retention of top-notch managers and advisors. Far too many financial institutions have tried to build programs on the cheap, not understanding the benefits that a stable, experienced core of investment professionals can bring. Sovereign funds that have not been willing or able to bring in a successful investment team would have been far better off had they simply put their capital into index funds that track the market.

Consider, for instance, a number of state pension funds in the United States. Not only are salary levels far below comparable rewards in the private sector, but there are too few efforts to make the work rewarding. Rather than emphasize the broad mission of the investment office, administrators often limit the discretion of investment professionals. Recommendations of the staff are all too often overturned by a second-guessing investment committee. It is thus not surprising that many of these institutions are characterized by a revolving door, with employees lingering just long enough to become attractive to employers in the private sector.

Adequately compensating personnel is, of course, easier said than done. A tremendous distaste surrounds the payment of "excessive" compensation to those in the public trust. But if sovereign wealth funds are going to ask their staffs to play roles akin to those of private equity investors—and expect to recruit and retain skilled professionals—adjusting compensation schedules to more clearly mirror those in the private sector is essential.

This mission can be particularly difficult in democracies, where the media may misrepresent compensation arrangements. Consider, for instance, In-Q-Tel, which, while not a sovereign fund, dramatically illustrates this problem.

In-Q-Tel was established in 1999 to give the U.S. Central Intelligence Agency greater access to cutting-edge technologies.[17] At the time of its establishment, the U.S. intelligence community realized it was being overwhelmed: not only had the volume of Internet and telephone communication exploded to the point where it was impossible to monitor, but the nation had to worry about many more enemies than in the Cold War days. The agency's scientific leaders also realized that the most sophisticated technologies were being developed not within government laboratories, but rather in Silicon Valley start-ups. Brilliant engineers that in earlier days might have been lured to work in advanced government facilities were instead streaming to young firms in the hopes of hitting it rich.

In-Q-Tel was designed to address this problem by allowing the government to access some of the key innovations in these firms. Using a variety of venture-like tools, the organization invested modest stakes in emerging companies, often in conjunction with independent venture firms. It also served as a bridge, introducing firms in its portfolio to the intelligence community and highlighting the government as an important new customer for their products. For many of the start-ups, which had targeted corporate customers, the challenges of breaking

176

into government procurement were daunting. For instance, Las Vegas–based Systems Research and Development employed "Non-Obvious Relationship Analysis" to allow casinos to identify card counters and cheaters. Jeff Jonas, the firm's chief executive officer, considered selling the technology to the government for national security applications, but noted, "It was very hard to be a West Coast company that's never done anything in Washington, with no visibility or awareness into sensitive federal agencies. You can't just show up from Vegas and say 'So you want to buy a watch?'"[18]

The CIA realized it needed a special kind of team to run In-Q-Tel: individuals who were at once conversant with the world of high-technology start-ups and with a ponderous, security-conscious government bureaucracy. To maximize the chance of getting the right people, the CIA set up In-Q-Tel as an independent, not-for-profit entity, which shielded it from civil service rules that might discourage many recruits. While the agency believed the primary lure for working at In-Q-Tel would be the opportunity to fund cutting-edge technologies and to help the nation, there was also a need for a diverse array of people at the fund. For every gray-haired executive who had already struck it rich in high technology, there should be several younger associates. In order to attract these staff members—and to avoid a revolving door through which people left as soon as they had the requisite experience—the CIA designed a compensation scheme quite different from that in typical government jobs. The package included a flat salary, a bonus based on how well In-Q-Tel met government needs, and an employee investment program, which took a prespecified portion of each employee's salary and invested alongside In-Q-Tel in the young firms in its portfolio. With this arrangement, In-Q-Tel was able to attract a strong team, including, as CEO, Gilman Louie, a twenty-year veteran of Silicon Valley and head of a number of successful game companies.

After a few years of operations, however, the *New York Post*—a newspaper better known for covering the barroom and bedroom escapades of actresses, politicians, and ballplayers—decided to turn its attention to In-Q-Tel.[19] Describing it as "an astonishing tale of taxpayer-financed intrigue on capitalism's street of dreams," journalists homed in on the compensation scheme: one article charged that In-Q-Tel employees

177

were "speculat[ing] with taxpayer money for their own personal benefit." Needless to say, there was no discussion of the challenges of recruiting investment staff conversant with Silicon Valley, or the likelihood that many In-Q-Tel professionals could make far more in the
private sector. This arrangement, the *Post* intoned, was "almost identical to the so-called 'Raptor' partnerships through which top officials at
Enron Corp were able to cash in personally on investment activities of
the very company that employed them." (Never mind that such arrangements have also been used by many of the best corporate venture
partnerships . . .)

While In-Q-Tel continues, Gilman Louie himself in early 2006
began his own venture capital fund with seasoned investor Stewart Al-
sopp. His colleague Mark Frantz, a managing general partner at In-Q-
Tel, left about the same time to become general partner with Reston,
Virginia's Redshift Ventures, formerly known as SpaceVest. Whether it
was compensation levels—which while attractive by government standards, were far below those of independent venture capitalists—the
distractions associated with frequent congressional investigations, or
the media scrutiny, In-Q-Tel has struggled to hold onto its investment
staff, despite a creative attempt to create attractive incentives.

These problems are not unique to democracies, though. A number
of sovereign funds in other nations have suffered from a brain drain
as the most experienced operatives have left to begin their own firms
or join independent groups. In these cases, the crucial limitation has
been not the fear of a crusading press, but rather reluctance by government leaders to offer pay that might be perceived as unfair or
disruptive.

In short, the need to view the development of a sovereign wealth
fund as an investment is critical. Just as with a public building project,
these offices require careful planning and the recruitment and retention of top-tier staff. In this area, enduring success comes not to the
lucky, but rather to those who take a thoughtful approach!

Go small. A final point is to emulate smaller institutions. In extreme
cases, the size of sovereign funds can be so great that a kind of paralysis
sets in. To have the probability of contributing meaningfully to returns, each investment needs to be so large that smaller investments

don't get made, even if collectively they would have a substantial impact. And it may be that the very large investments the fund does get offered are not the best ones.

One way around this constriction is to build an organizational structure in which a number of subsidiaries are managed separately. In this way, managers can make smaller investments, secure in the knowledge that if successful, they will affect their own performance. Such separate funds can also serve as "laboratories": successful approaches can be emulated by the other funds, while mistakes can be less costly since they affect only one subsidiary. (This approach resembles the "skunk works" and corporate venturing programs that major technology firms have employed in their research laboratories.)

Several illustrations of such an approach can be pointed to. For instance, since 1960, Sweden has operated a number of independent pension funds.[20] Now numbering seven in total, the funds were envisioned as operating independently, on mutually competitive terms. Each fund, in theory, is allowed to formulate its own investment approaches, corporate governance policies, and risk management strategies. While the Swedish regulators have not allowed as much competition as might be desired—the funds have had to keep a chunk of their assets in bonds, and been strictly limited in the amount of alternative investments they can hold—the idea of fostering competition between funds is a laudable one. In a somewhat similar spirit, the Government of Singapore Investment Corporation has established separate subsidiaries for asset management (liquid investments), real estate, and special investments, each with its own chairman, board, and president.[21]

FINAL THOUGHTS

In many respects, the challenges associated with managing sovereign wealth funds are similar to those facing other public venture initiatives. Because they often operate in the public spotlight, decisions must be made with a complex set of goals in mind and in the face of external pressures.

But in two key respects, the management of sovereign funds poses

179

unique issues. First, the quantity of capital these groups invest is in many instances massive, which limits their flexibility in pursuing new opportunities. Second, the intense interest in—and in some cases, fear of—sovereign wealth funds in many Western nations increases the difficulty of fulfilling their already challenging missions.

In this chapter, we have explored the complex world of sovereign wealth funds. We have acknowledged that demands for visibility pose a problem for which we have no good solution. Such disclosures—while perhaps necessary from a political perspective—are likely to make the funds' goals harder to achieve. But the process of managing increasingly large amounts of capital can be addressed. The best practices of endowments and other seasoned institutions illustrate how to manage substantial assets while maintaining a clear focus.

CHAPTER 9

LESSONS AND PITFALLS

The stories and studies discussed in earlier chapters have a variety of implications for those—whether government officials, local business leaders, or simply interested citizens—who seek to promote high-potential entrepreneurship and venture capital. While in many cases this evidence illustrates what not to do, it also offers many positive suggestions.

In this final chapter, I highlight a number of implications that emerge from the earlier discussions. I also discuss frequently offered suggestions and programs to boost entrepreneurial and venture capital activity that are less consistent with the principles outlined in this book, and explain why they do not make sense.

RECOMMENDED RULES OF THUMB

There are a number of important guidelines that, if followed, would facilitate the development of local entrepreneurial and venture capital activity:

- *Remember that entrepreneurial activity does not exist in a vacuum.* Entrepreneurs are tremendously dependent on their partners. Without experienced lawyers able to negotiate agreements, skilled marketing gurus and engineers who are willing to work for low wages and a handful of stock options, and customers who are willing to take a chance on a young firm, success is unlikely. But despite the importance of the entrepreneurial environment, in many cases government officials hand out money without thinking about barriers other than money that entrepreneurs face. In some cases, crucial aspects of the entrepreneurial environment may seem tangential: for instance, the importance of robust public markets for young firms as a spur to venture investment (as noted in chapter 5). Singapore provides a great example of a nation that took a broad view and addressed not just the availability of capital, but other components needed to create a productive arena in which entrepreneurs could operate.

- *Leverage the local academic scientific and research base.* One particular precondition to entrepreneurship deserves special mention: in many regions of the world, there is a mismatch between the low level of entrepreneurial activity and venture capital financing, on the one hand, and the strength of the scientific and research base, on the other. The role of technology transfer offices is absolutely critical here. Effective offices do not just license technologies, but also educate nascent academic entrepreneurs and introduce them to venture investors. Building the capabilities of local technology transfer offices, and training both potential academic entrepreneurs and technology transfer personnel in the process of new firm formation, is essential. All too often, technology transfer offices are encouraged to maximize the short-run return from licensing transactions. This leads to an emphasis on transactions with established corporations that can make substantial up-front payments, even though licensing new technologies to start-ups can yield substantial returns in the long run, both to the institution and to the region as a whole. It is important that policymakers think seriously about the way in which technology transfer is being undertaken, the incentives being offered, and their consequences.

- *Respect the need for conformity to global standards.* It is natural to want to hold onto long-standing approaches in matters such as securities regulation and taxes. In many cases, these approaches have evolved to address specific problems, and have proven to be effective. Nevertheless, there is a strong case for adopting the de facto global standards. Global institutional investors and venture funds are likely to be discouraged if customary partnership and preferred stock structures cannot be employed in a given nation. Even if a perfectly good alternative exists, they may be unwilling to devote the time and resources to explore it. Unless the nation is one such as China—where global investors feel compelled to master the system, no matter how complex, owing to the size of the market opportunity—policymakers should allow transactions that conform to the models widely accepted as best practice.

- *Let the market provide direction.* Two successful efforts have been the Israeli Yozma program and the New Zealand Seed Investment Fund. While these programs differed in their details—the former was geared toward attracting foreign venture investors; the latter encouraged locally based, early-stage funds—they shared a central element: each used matching funds to determine where public subsidies should go. In using the market for guidance, policymakers should keep certain points in mind:

  - The identification of appropriate firms or funds is not likely to take place overnight. Rather than fund dozens of groups immediately, programs should first fund a handful of entities. As feedback comes in from the early participants, second and third batches of capital may be invested, or the capital of the pioneering firms and funds may be supplemented.

  - These initiatives should not compete with independent venture funds or finance substandard firms that cannot raise private capital. Emulating successful initiatives in the past, programs should require that a substantial amount of funds be raised from nonpublic sources.

  - In selecting venture funds to which to provide capital, it may be a challenge to interest top-tier venture groups. The expectation should be that a given region can attract solid groups with a particular interest in industries where there is already real local strength.

183

- In the same spirit, policymakers may wish to cast their net broadly to attract firms and funds of different types. In addition to traditional stand-alone start-up venture funds, they may wish to consider corporate spin-outs and venture funds as well.

- In encouraging seed companies and groups, leaders should be aware that extensive intervention may be needed before they are "fund-able." Programs may need to work closely with the organizations to refine strategies, recruit additional partners (perhaps even from other regions), and identify potential investors. Moreover, firms and groups should retain enough "dry powder" so that they do not go belly-up once government subsidies run out. Having the right leader is critical if a program's interventions are to be effective.

- Policymakers should publicize in advance their evaluation criteria for prospective firms and funds. These evaluation standards should be close to those employed in the private sector for assessing entrepreneurs and venture funds.

- *Resist the temptation to overengineer.* In many instances, government requirements that limit the flexibility of entrepreneurs and venture investors have been detrimental. It is tempting to add restrictions on several dimensions: for instance, the locations in which the firms can operate, the type of securities venture investors can use, and the evolution of the firms (e.g., restrictions on acquisitions or secondary sales of stock). Government programs should eschew such efforts to micromanage the entrepreneurial process. While it is natural to expect that firms and groups receiving subsidies will retain a local presence or continue to target the local region for investments, these requirements should be as minimal as possible.

- *Recognize the long lead times associated with public venture initiatives.* One of the common failings of public entrepreneurship and venture capital initiatives has been impatience. Building an entrepreneurial sector is a long-run endeavor, not an overnight accomplishment. Programs that have initial promise should be given time to prove their merits. Far too often, promising initiatives have been abandoned on the basis of partial (and often, not the most critical) indicators: for instance, low interim rates of return of initial participants. Impatience—or creating rules that force program participants to focus on short-run returns—is a recipe for failure.

- *Avoid initiatives that are too large or too small.* Policymakers must walk a tightrope in finding the appropriate size for venture initiatives. Too small a program will do little to improve the environment for pioneering entrepreneurs and venture funds. Moreover, inflated expectations, out of proportion to the money invested, may create a backlash that impedes future efforts. But programs that are too substantial can swamp local markets. The imbalance between plentiful capital and limited opportunities may introduce pathologies. Consider the Canadian Labor Fund Program discussed in chapter 6. Not only did it back incompetent groups that did little to spur entrepreneurship, but it crowded out some of the most knowledgeable local investors.

- *Understand the importance of global interconnections.* As this book has repeatedly emphasized, entrepreneurship and venture capital are emerging as global enterprises. This evolution has two important consequences. First, no matter how eager policymakers are to encourage activity in their own backyard, they must realize that to be successful, firms must have a multinational presence. Efforts to restrict firms to hiring and manufacturing locally are likely to be self-defeating. Second, it is important to involve overseas investors as much as feasible. Local companies can benefit from relationships with funds based elsewhere but investing capital locally. Moreover, successful investments will attract more overseas capital. In addition, local affiliates of a fund based elsewhere—having a successful track record—will gain the credibility they need to raise their own funds. That being said, when public funds subsidize activities by overseas parties, officials should

185

obtain commitments from these entrepreneurs and groups to re-cruit personnel to be resident locally, and to have partners based elsewhere be involved with the management of the local groups.

- *Institutionalize careful evaluations of initiatives.* All too often, in the rush to boost entrepreneurship, policymakers make no provision for the evaluation of programs. The future of initiatives should be determined by their success or failure in meeting their goals, rather than other considerations (such as the vehemence with which supporters argue for their continuation). Careful program evaluations will help ensure better decisions. These evaluations should consider not just the individual funds and companies participating in the programs, but also the broader context. At the very least, these evaluations should:

  - Gather and publicize accurate data on the extent of high-potential entrepreneurship and formal and informal venture capital activity. Some of this information can be collected immediately; other information can only be gathered after some activity. These data will be important not only for the program evaluations, but also to publicize the growing size and dynamism of the local venture market to prospective investors.

  - Compare publicly supported firms and venture groups to their peers to infer the difference the program has made.

  - Carefully track the performance of the companies that are and are not participating in the program, including not just financial returns but also such elements as sales and employment growth.

  Evaluators may also wish to consider whether it would be feasible to randomize at least some awards, or explore the use of regression discontinuity analysis in the evaluations.

- *Realize that programs need creativity and flexibility.* Too often, public venturing initiatives are like the pock-faced villain in a horror film—as much as one tries, he cannot be killed off! Their seeming immortality reflects the capture problem discussed in chapter 4: powerful vested interests coalesce behind initiatives, making them impossible to get rid of. The nations that have been most successful in public programs have been willing to end those that are not doing well, and to substitute other incentives. Even more powerfully, they have been willing to end programs on the grounds that they are *too* successful and hence no longer in need of public funding. Moreover, program rules may have to evolve, even if important classes of participants are thereby eliminated. If government is going to be in the business of promoting entrepreneurship, it needs some entrepreneurial qualities itself.

- *Recognize that "agency problems" are universal and take steps to minimize their danger.* The stories in this volume illustrate that the temptations to direct public subsidies in ways not intended are not confined to any region, political system, or ethnicity. While we might wish that human beings everywhere would confine themselves to maximizing public welfare, selfish interest all too often rears its ugly head. In designing public programs to promote venture capital and entrepreneurship, such behavior should be limited as far as possible. Defining and adhering to clear strategies and procedures for venture initiatives, creating a firewall between elected officials and program administrators, and careful assessments of the program can help limit self-serving behavior.

- *Make education an important part of the mixture.* The emphasis on education should have at least three dimensions:

  - The first is building the understanding of outsiders about the local market's potential. One of the critical barriers to willingness of venture investors to invest in a given nation is a lack of information. If one visits a racetrack for the first time, it's always nice to know whether the track favors front-runners or late closers, and who the hot local jockeys are. In the same way, institutions feel more comfortable investing if they have information about the level of entrepreneurial activity in local markets, the outcomes of the investments, and so forth. An important role that government can play is gathering this information, or else encouraging (and perhaps funding) a local trade association to do so.

- Second, educating entrepreneurs is a critical process. In many emerging venture markets, entrepreneurs may have a great deal of confidence, but relatively little understanding of the expectations of top-tier private investors, potential strategic partners, and investment bankers. The more that can be done to fill these gaps, the better.

- Finally, a broad-based understanding in the public sector of the challenges of entrepreneurial and venture capital development is very helpful. As we have repeatedly highlighted, policymakers have made expensive errors out of a lack of understanding of how these markets really work.

APPROACHES SOMETIMES RECOMMENDED THAT SHOULD BE AVOIDED

Not all the suggestions that circulate in policy circles are good ones. In this section, we'll consider some ideas that are frequently heard—indeed, often touted by consultants and intermediaries—but are inconsistent with the global evidence on appropriate steps to build a successful entrepreneurial sector or venture capital.

- *Go domestic.* Local entrepreneurs and venture investors frequently demand that government funds—whether sovereign funds owned by the states or pension funds for public employees—be mandated to devote their general investment pool to domestic entrepreneurs or venture funds. This suggestion, while initially plausible, is problematic for several reasons.

    First, the success of dynamic markets is largely driven by the engagement of global private equity limited partners, rather than local players. Early-stage venture funds—assuming that they can develop a reasonable track record—are likely to attract considerable interest from institutional investors. By directing funds to local groups that cannot raise money, governments are likely to be rewarding precisely the groups that don't deserve funds.

Moreover, a real danger with public programs is that they flood the market with far more capital than it can deploy. Such well-intentioned steps can actually hurt entrepreneurs and venture capitalists.

Finally, rules requiring local investment fly in the face of the principle that public venture capital funds should rely on the market to identify attractive opportunities, rather invent their own mandates. While it would be hoped that local pension and investment funds will eventually play an important role in local markets, it should be at a pace that they are comfortable with.

- *Set up immediate tax breaks.* A second bad idea is the commonly heard demand for provisions that give venture capital investors an immediate tax deduction. A frequently cited model is the CAPCO program pioneered in Louisiana and adopted by other states. Unfortunately, as discussed in chapter 7, these efforts have been largely unsuccessful.

  This suggestion is problematic for two reasons. First, the primary way in which tax policy encourages venture capital is through the demand side: the incentive that the entrepreneur has to (typically) quit a salaried job and begin a new firm. Little evidence suggests that tax policy can dramatically affect the amount of venture capital supplied by the sophisticated institutional investors that provide capital to the world's leading venture industries. (Indeed, many dominant venture capital investors—such as pension funds and endowments—are exempt from taxes in most nations.)

  Second, one of the powerful features of the venture capital process is the alignment of incentives. No one—whether limited partner, venture capitalist, or entrepreneur—gets substantial gains until the company is sold or goes public. Economists argue that such an alignment keeps everyone focused and minimizes the danger of behavior that benefits one party but hurts the firm. Sub-

189

stantial tax incentives at the time of the investment can distort this alignment of incentives.

- *Bring in hired guns with poor incentives.* Another bad idea, tried in a number of American states, is to bring in an outside investment firm to manage the entrepreneurship promotion initiative. For several reasons this decision will probably be unproductive. First, these intermediaries frequently charge substantial fees. While they may appear small (only 1 percent of capital under management!), they can eat up a huge fraction of the returns.

  Second, the investments by the intermediary may not be driven by the local government's priorities. The intermediary's fees can create incentives to do deals for their own sake, rather than to advance the mission of the fund. Thus, an outside financial institution may be tempted to put money to work quickly, so it can raise another fund (and generate more fees). Alternatively, the intermediary may have a special relationship with certain funds (for instance, an investment bank's fund-raising group may be gathering capital for that group). Divided loyalties will come into play, and the best interests of the government may not be served. Thus, U.S. states such as Oklahoma that have hired outside managers to run their entrepreneurship programs have had limited success in growing their venture sectors.

- *Imitation is the sincerest form of flattery.* Another persistent theme—perhaps the hardest to resist—is the desirability of duplicating programs and incentives provided elsewhere. In chapter 1, we discussed the temptation of so many Persian Gulf states to borrow concepts from Dubai, even though the very fact that the strategies (such as the creation of a major air travel hub) were successful for Dubai means that they are less likely to work elsewhere.

  Moreover, there has been a strong temptation to emulate even programs that have proved unsuccessful elsewhere. For instance, incentive schemes that give large tax benefits for those who invest in entrepreneurial firms have typically been unsuccessful in promoting entrepreneurship, yet have been widely emulated. Similarly, the widely adopted strategy of instructing local pension fund

190

managers to make economically targeted investments with employees' funds has a troubled legacy.

It is important to remember the adage "Two wrongs do not make a right." Ill-considered steps to promote entrepreneurship and venture capital can be profoundly distorting, attracting inexperienced operators and leading to ill-fated investments. The poisonous legacy that results can discourage other legitimate investors from participating in the market for years to come and set back the creation of a healthy industry. Thus, tempting as it is to match investment incentives offered by others, if a strategy appears ill-considered, it is best avoided.

FINAL THOUGHTS

In this book we began by highlighting the extraordinary recent public expenditures devoted to rescuing troubled firms, and asked whether government should have a role in the promotion of newer, more promising firms as well. We then looked at the experiences in encouraging entrepreneurs and venture capitalists across many decades and continents. We have delved into theoretical models and empirical studies. We have seen the good, the bad, and the ugly.

As I acknowledged in the introduction, the quest to encourage venture activity can seem like a sideshow among the many responsibilities of government, from waging war to ensuring the stability of major financial institutions. Certainly, the dollars spent each year on entrepreneurship programs—while significant on an absolute basis—pale when compared to defense and health care expenditures. But the picture changes when we consider the long-run consequences of policies that facilitate or hinder the development of a venture sector: that is, the impact on national prosperity of a vital entrepreneurial climate. In the long run, the significance of entrepreneurial policies looms much larger.

Much of the discussion in the book has focused on specific policies and analyses. But throughout the discussion, five consistent themes have emerged:

191

- Governments around the world today seek to promote entrepreneurial and venture capital activity, employing a variety of "stage setting" and direct strategies.

- These steps are sensible, given the historical record and theoretical arguments regarding the importance of such interventions in the development of entrepreneurial regions and industries.

- But programs to promote entrepreneurship are challenging. Governments cannot dictate how a venture market will evolve, and top-down efforts are likely to be unsuccessful.

- The same common flaws doom far too many programs. These flaws reflect both poor design—indicating a lack of understanding of the entrepreneurial process—and poor implementation.

- Governments must do a careful balancing act, combining an understanding of the necessity of their catalytic role with an awareness of the limits of their ability to stimulate the entrepreneurial sector.

If policymakers apply these key lessons, many sagas of waste and disappointment can be avoided. Entrepreneurs will find a more hospitable climate, and we will all benefit from a healthier economic world.

NOTES

PREFACE

1. See Tor Klette, Jarle Moen, and Zvi Griliches, "Do Subsidies to Commercial R&D Reduce Market Failures? Microeconomic Evaluation Studies," *Research Policy* 29 (2000): 471–95, for an overview of the current state of empirical research in this area.

CHAPTER 1: INTRODUCTION

1. "AIG Gets $150 Billion Government Bailout; Posts Huge Loss," Reuters News Service, November 10, 2008, and Nelson D. Schwartz, "UBS Given an Infusion of Capital," *New York Times*, October 16, 2008.

2. The Global Entrepreneurship Monitor's tabulations are available at "The Global Entrepreneurship Monitor," http://www.gemcon sortium.org/ (accessed July 11, 2008). It should be noted that the results of these and similar comparisons, which rely on surveys with different sampling methodologies and survey responses in different languages across countries, must be viewed with some caution.

3. This account is based on *Economist*, "Dubai: Facts and Figures," http://www.economist.com/cities/findStory.cfm?CITY_ID=DUB &FOLDER=Facts-History (accessed August 10, 2008) and related articles; Ali Tawfik Al Sadik, "Evolution and Performance of the UAE Economy, 1972–1998," in *United Arab Emirates: A New Perspective*, ed. Ibrahim Abed and Peter Hellyer (London: Trident Press, 2001), 202–30; and William Goetzmann and Irina Tarris, "Dubailand: Destination Dubai," *Harvard Business School Case* (2007): no. 9-207-005.

4. This account is based, among other sources, on Jacques Horovitz and Anne-Valerie Ohlsson, "Dubai Internet City: Serving Business,"

IMD Case (2005): no. 224; and Daron K. Roberts, Inder Singh, and Johnny Vong, *Dubai Internet City as a Policy Intervention for ICT Growth: An Analysis of Dubai's Strategy to Cultivate an ICT Cluster,* unpublished Policy Analysis Exercise, John F. Kennedy School of Government, Harvard University, 2004.

5. See, for instance, Chip Cummings, "Dubai's Debt Cloud," *Wall Street Journal,* December 14, 2007; Stanley Reed, "The Downturn Hits Dubai," *Business Week Online,* December 3, 2008, http://www.businessweek.com/globalbiz/content/dec2008/gb2008123_682864.htm?chan=top+news_top+news+index+-+temp_news+%2B+analysis (accessed February 11, 2009); and Robert F. Worth, "Laid-Off Foreigners Flee as Dubai Spirals Down," *New York Times,* February 11, 2009.

6. For overviews of economic policies in Jamaica and Singapore, see Owen Jefferson, *Stabilization and Stagnation in the Jamaican Economy, 1972–97: Some Reflections on Macroeconomic Policy over the Past Twenty-five Years* (Kingston: University of the West Indies, 1999); and Koh Ai Tee, ed., *The Singapore Economy in the 21st Century: Issues and Strategies* (New York: McGraw-Hill, 2002). This section has benefited greatly from conversations with Peter Henry, as well as from his white paper, "The Jamaican Economy: Maintaining Stability and Moving to Growth," working paper, Stanford University, 2006.

7. These figures are computed using the Central Intelligence Agency, *2008 World Factbook* (Langley, VA: CIA, 2008); Council of Economic Advisors, Executive Office of the President, *2008 Economic Report of the President* (Washington, D.C.: Government Printing Office, 2008); and the World Bank's World Development Indicators database.

8. Vanetta Skeete, Claudette Williams-Myers, Olusegun Afis Ismail, and Sandra Glasgow, *Global Entrepreneurship Monitor: 2006 Jamaica Report* (Kingston: University of Technology, 2007).

9. Sandra Glasgow, Claudette Williams-Myers, Vanetta Skeete, and Olusegun Afis Ismail, *Global Entrepreneurship Monitor: 2005 Jamaica Report* (Kingston: University of Technology, 2006).

10. International Finance Corporation, "Doing Business: Jamaica,"

http://www.doingbusiness.org/ExploreEconomies/?economyid=97 (accessed August 8, 2008).

11. International Finance Corporation, "Doing Business: Singapore," http://www.doingbusiness.org/ExploreEconomies/?economyid =167 (accessed August 8, 2008).

12. International Finance Corporation, "Doing Business: United States," http://www.doingbusiness.org/ExploreEconomies/?economyid =197 (accessed August 8, 2008).

13. Henry, "The Jamaican Economy," 12.

CHAPTER 2: A LOOK BACKWARDS

1. This figure is compiled from various publications and web sites of the Canadian, European, Israeli, and U.S. (National) venture capital associations, as well as those of the Asian Venture Capital Journal. In some nations where venture capital investments are not clearly delineated, I employ seed and start-up investments.

2. The sources for the 1996 chart are the same as those in figure 2.1. The 2007 chart is based on Ernst & Young, *Innovation: The Growing Importance of Venture Capital: Global Venture Capital Insights and Trends Report, 2008* (New York: Ernst & Young, 2008) and the European Private Equity and Venture Capital Association, *EVCA 2008 Yearbook* (Brussels: European Private Equity and Venture Capital Association, 2008). Ernst & Young's definitions of venture activity differ somewhat from the other sources, and hence the 2007 data in figures 2.1 and 2.2 are not completely consistent.

3. See William R. Kerr, "Ethnic Scientific Communities and International Technology Diffusion," *Review of Economics and Statistics* 90 (2008): 518–37.

4. This figure was compiled from the web site and publications of SDC Venture Economics.

5. See, for instance, Linda Himelstein, "Squabbling among the Rich and Famous: After Months of Fighting, 12 Entrepreneuring Is in Trouble," *Business Week* 3759 (November 26, 2001): 72–73; Stefan

Krempl, "We Will Survive," *Financial Times*, May 25, 2001; and Simon English, "Internet Entrepreneur Celebrates Pounds 61m Deal," *Independent*, May 11, 2006.

6. The time series in this figure is taken from various editions of the Asian Venture Capital Journal's *Asian Private Equity 300 Guide* and *Guide to Venture Capital in Asia*.

7. This account is drawn from Henny Sender, "China Tries Venture Capitalism—the Government Emulates Western Counterparts—Its Own Way—Having Missed the Industrial Revolution, They Can't Afford to Miss This One, Says Singaporean Partner," *Asian Wall Street Journal*, January 3, 2001; and Feng Zeng, "Venture Capital Investments in China," Ph.D. diss., Pardee Rand Graduate School, 2004.

8. Felda Hardymon, Ann Leamon, and Josh Lerner, "Chengwei Ventures and the hdt* Investment," *Harvard Business School Case* (2002): no. 9-802-089.

9. T. J. Rodgers, *Why Silicon Valley Should Not Normalize Relations with Washington D.C.* (Washington, D.C.: Cato Institute, 2000), 2–9.

10. While there are a substantial number of histories of Silicon Valley, most helpful in the preparation of this account were Stuart W. Leslie and Robert H. Kargon, "Selling Silicon Valley: Frederick Terman's Model for Regional Advantage," *Business History Review* 70 (1996): 435–72; Annalee Saxenien, *Regional Advantage: Culture and Competition in Silicon Valley and Route 128* (Cambridge: Harvard University Press, 1994); and especially Timothy J. Sturgeon, "How Silicon Valley Came to Be," in *Understanding the Silicon Valley: Anatomy of an Entrepreneurial Region*, ed. Martin Kenney (Stanford: Stanford University Press, 2000), 15–47.

11. Sturgeon, "Silicon Valley," 16.

12. Ibid., 17–23.

13. Leslie and Kargon, "Selling Silicon Valley," 419.

14. For systematic evidence of the importance of spin-offs in Silicon Valley, see Paul Gompers, Josh Lerner, and David Scharfstein, "Entrepreneurial Spawning: Public Corporations and the Genesis of New Ventures, 1986 to 1999," *Journal of Finance* 60 (2005): 577–614.

15. Sturgeon, "Silicon Valley," 30–34.

16. Ibid., 34 and 45–46.

17. Saxenien, *Regional Advantage*, 21.

18. This paragraph is largely based on ibid., 22–23.

19. For one discussion of the limitations of public efforts to boost entrepreneurial firms in the 1920s, see Joseph L. Nicholson, "The Fallacy of Easy Money for Small Business," *Harvard Business Review* 17:1 (Autumn 1938): 31–34.

20. This history of American Research and Development is largely drawn from Spencer Ante, *Creative Capital: Georges Doriot and the Birth of Venture Capital* (Boston: Harvard Business School Press, 2008); and Patrick R. Liles, *Sustaining the Venture Capital Firm* (Cambridge, Mass.: Management Analysis Center, 1978).

21. Ralph Flanders, "The Problem of Development Capital," *Commercial and Financial Chronicle* 162:4442 (November 29, 1945): 2576, 2608.

22. Liles, *Venture Capital Firm*, 32.

23. Gene Bylinsky, "General Doriot's Dream Factory," *Fortune* 76:2 (August 1967): 103–36.

24. This history of the SBIC program is drawn from C. M. Noone and S. M. Rubel, *SBICs: Pioneers in Organized Venture Capital* (Chicago: Capital Publishing, 1970); Jonathan J. Bean, *Big Government and Affirmative Action: The Scandalous History of the Small Business Administration* (Lexington: University Press of Kentucky, 2001); and Liles, *Venture Capital Firm*.

25. Bean, *Big Government*, 56.

26. See the discussion, for instance, in Vyvyan Tenorio, "SBA's Dilemma: Troubled VCs," *Daily Deal*, September 9, 2002; and Bean, *Big Government*.

27. Timothy Bates, "The Minority Enterprise Small Business Investment Company Program: Institutionalizing a Nonviable Minority Business Assistance Infrastructure," *Urban Affairs Review* 32 (1997): 683–703.

28. This history is based on Felda Hardymon, Ann Leamon, and Josh Lerner, "3i Group PLC," *Harvard Business School Case* (2003): no. 9-803-020; "3i, Fifty Years of Growth: 1945–1995," private document; and Richard Coopey and Donald Clarke, *3i: Fifty Years Investing in Industry* (Oxford: Oxford University Press, 1995).

CHAPTER 3: WHY SHOULD POLICYMAKERS CARE?

1. Morris Abramowitz, "Resource and Output Trends in the United States since 1870," *American Economic Review* 46 (1956): 5–23.

2. Robert M. Solow, "Technical Change and the Aggregate Production Function," *Review of Economics and Statistics* 39 (1957): 312–20.

3. The interested reader can turn to surveys by Pierre Azoulay and Josh Lerner, "Technological Innovation and Organizations," in *Handbook of Organizational Economics*, ed. Robert Gibbons and John Roberts (Princeton: Princeton University Press, forthcoming); and Wesley M. Cohen and Richard C. Levin, "Empirical Studies of Innovation and Market Structure," in *Handbook of Industrial Organization*, vol. 2, ed. Richard Schmalensee and Robert D. Willig (New York: North-Holland, 1989), chap. 18.

4. Wesley M. Cohen, Richard C. Levin, and David C. Mowery, "Firm Size and R&D Intensity: A Re-examination," *Journal of Industrial Economics* 35 (1987): 543–63.

5. Zoltan J. Acs and David B. Audretsch, "Innovation in Large and Small Firms: An Empirical Analysis," *American Economic Review* 78 (1988): 678–90.

6. John Jewkes, David Sawers, and Richard Stillerman, *The Sources of Invention* (New York: St. Martin's Press, 1958).

7. The first example of the arguments along these lines I am aware of is Richard N. Foster, *Innovation: The Attackers' Advantage* (London: Macmillan, 1986).

8. See, for instance, Debra J. Aron and Edward P. Lazear, "The Introduction of New Products," *American Economic Review Papers and Proceedings* 80 (1990): 421–26.

9. Thomas J. Prusa and James A. Schmitz Jr., "Can Companies Maintain Their Initial Innovation Thrust? A Study of the PC Software Industry," *Review of Economics and Statistics* 76 (1994): 523–40.

10. This account is based on, among other sources, Felda Hardymon and Ann Leamon, "Celtel International B.V.," *Harvard Business School Case* (2006): no. 9-805-061; Ian Giddy, "The Acquisition of Celtel An African Company's choice: IPO or Sale," *New York University Case* (2007): unnumbered, posted at http://pages.stern.nyu.edu/

~igiddy/cases/mtc-celtel.htm (accessed October 15, 2008); Fundamo, "Celplay Zambia Upgrades Technology to Directly Answer African Population Requirements," http://www.fundamo.com/article14.aspx (accessed October 9, 2008).

11. Zain, "Mobile Telephony to Reach 400,000 People in Remote African Villages," http://www.zain.com/muse/obj/lang.default/portal .view/content/Media%20centre/Press%20releases/AfricaMillennium Villages (accessed October 8, 2008).

12. William A. Wells, "Venture Capital Decision Making." Ph.D. diss., Carnegie-Mellon University, 1974.

13. David Amis and Howard Stevenson, *Winning Angels* (New York: Pearson Education Limited, 2001), 114.

14. T. T. Tyebjee and A. V. Bruno, "A Model of Venture Capitalist Investment Activity," *Management Science* 30 (1984): 1051–66.

15. Steven N. Kaplan and Per Stromberg, "Characteristics, Contracts, and Actions: Evidence from Venture Capitalist Analyses," *Journal of Finance* 109 (2004): 2173–2206.

16. Paul Gompers and Josh Lerner, *The Venture Capital Cycle* (Cambridge: MIT Press, 1999).

17. Wells, "Venture Capital Decision Making," 47; and George W. Fenn, Nellie Liang, and Stephen Prowse, *The Economics of the Private Equity Market* (Washington, D.C.: Federal Reserve Board, 1996).

18. Bessemer Venture Partners, "Anti-Portfolio," http://www.bvp .com/Portfolio/AntiPortfolio.aspx (accessed July 12, 2008).

19. Michael Gorman and William A. Sahlman, "What Do Venture Capitalists Do?" *Journal of Business Venturing* 4 (1989): 231–48.

20. This figure is based on the author's tabulation of unpublished data from SDC Venture Economics, with supplemental information from Compustat and the Center for Research into Securities Prices (CRSP) databases.

21. This discussion is based on James T. Areddy, "Venture Capital Swarms China," *Wall Street Journal*, March 14, 2006; "Chinese Startup Lingtu Collaborates with IBM to Reach New Markets," *PR Newswire*, June 28, 2006; Felda Hardymon and Ann Leamon, "Gobi Partners: Raising Fund II," *Harvard Business School Case* (2007): no. 9-807-093; and conversations with key practitioners.

22. Hardymon and Leamon, "Gobi Partners," 9.

23. Ibid.

24. The discussion is based on Abraaj Capital, *Annual Report* (Dubai: Abraaj, 2008); Ant Bozkaya and Josh Lerner, "Abraaj Capital," *Harvard Business School Case* (2008): no. 9-809-008; and Sarmad Khan, "Abraaj Sells Its Stake in National Air Services," *National (Dubai)*, June 17, 2008.

25. This figure is based on the author's tabulation of unpublished data from SDC Venture Economics, with supplemental information from Compustat and the Center for Research into Securities Prices (CRSP) databases.

26. Thomas Hellmann and Manju Puri, "The Interaction between Product Market and Financing Strategy: The Role of Venture Capital," *Review of Financial Studies* 13 (2000): 959–84.

27. Samuel S. Kortum and Josh Lerner, "Assessing the Contribution of Venture Capital to Innovation," *Rand Journal of Economics* 31 (2000): 674–92.

28. Patent applicants and examiners at the patent office include references to other relevant patents. These serve a legal role similar to that of property markers at the edge of a land holding.

CHAPTER 4: THINGS GET MORE COMPLICATED

1. This discussion is based primarily on Ernest Braun and Stuart MacDonald, *Revolution in Miniature: The History and Impact of Semiconductor Electronics Re-explored in an Updated and Revised Second Edition* (New York: Cambridge University Press, 1982); and Leslie R. Berlin, "Robert Noyce and Fairchild Semiconductor, 1957–1968," *Business History Review* 75 (2001): 63–101.

2. For a study of spawning in medical devices, see Aaron K. Chatterji, "Spawned with a Silver Spoon? Entrepreneurial Performance and Innovation in the Medical Device Industry," *Strategic Management Journal* (forthcoming); for a discussion of Recruit, see Josh Lerner, Lee Branstetter, and Takeshi Nakabayashi, "New Business In-

vestment Company: October 1997," *Harvard Business School Case* (1999): no. 9-299-025.

3. For a discussion of the benefits that deal-sharing can bring, see Josh Lerner, "The Syndication of Venture Capital Investments," *Financial Management* 23 (1994): 16–27.

4. These calculations are the author's. The database on which these calculations are based is described in Josh Lerner, Antoinette Schoar, and Wan Wongsunwai, "Smart Institutions, Foolish Choices: The Limited Partner Performance Puzzle," *Journal of Finance* 62 (2007): 731–64.

5. Liles, *Venture Capital Firm*, 83.

6. See the review in R. Glenn Hubbard, "Capital-Market Imperfections and Investment," *Journal of Economic Literature* 36 (1998): 193–225. Regarding the impact of capital constraints on investments in innovation, particularly helpful articles are Bronwyn H. Hall, "Investment and Research and Development: Does the Source of Financing Matter?" Working Paper No. 92-194, Department of Economics, University of California at Berkeley, 1992; Kenneth Y. Hao and Adam B. Jaffe, "Effect of Liquidity on Firms' R&D Spending," *Economics of Innovation and New Technology* 2 (1993): 275–82; and Charles P. Himmelberg and Bruce C. Petersen, "R&D and Internal Finance: A Panel Study of Small Firms in High-Tech Industries," *Review of Economics and Statistics* 76 (1994): 38–51.

7. Unless otherwise noted, numbers in this paragraph are taken from various yearbooks and the web site of the National Venture Capital Association.

8. U.S. Small Business Administration, *The Small Business Economy* (Washington, D.C.: Government Printing Office, 2007).

9. For an overview of the literature on herding by institutions, see Andrea Devenow and Ivo Welch, "Rational Herding in Financial Economics," *European Economic Review* 40 (1996): 603–15.

10. For a discussion of this argument, see David De Meza, "Overlending," *Economic Journal* 112 (2002): F17–F31.

11. See, for instance, Adam B. Jaffe, *Economic Analysis of Research Spillovers—Implications for the Advanced Technology Program* (Wash-

ington, D.C.: Advanced Technology Program, National Institute of Standards and Technology, U.S. Department of Commerce, 1996).

12. Zvi Griliches, "The Search for R&D Spillovers," *Scandinavian Journal of Economics* 94 (1992): S29–S47.

13. See, for instance, Jewkes, Sawers, and Stillerman, *The Sources of Invention*, and Edwin Mansfield, John Rapoport, Anthony Romeo, Samuel Wagner, and George Beardsley, "Social and Private Rates of Return from Industrial Innovations," *Quarterly Journal of Economics* 91 (1977): 221–40.

14. Douglass North, *Growth and Structural Change* (New York: Norton, 1981).

15. See, for instance, Alberto Alesina, Reza Baqir, and William Easterly, "Public Goods and Ethnic Divisions," working paper, Harvard University, 1997; and William Easterly and Ross Levine, "Africa's Growth Tragedy: Policies and Ethnic Divisions," *Quarterly Journal of Economics* 112 (1997): 1203–50.

16. For the classic paper in this literature, see Rafael La Porta, Florencio Lopez-de-Silanes, Andrei Shleifer, and Robert W. Vishny, "Law and Finance," *Journal of Political Economy* 106 (1998): 1113–55.

17. Rafael La Porta, Florencio Lopez-de-Silanes, Andrei Shleifer, and Robert W. Vishny, "The Quality of Government," *Journal of Law, Economics and Organization* 15 (2000): 222–79.

18. This account is based in part on Eli Noam, "Telecommunications in Transition," in *Changing the Rules: Technological Change, International Competition, and Regulation in Telecommunications*, ed. Robert W. Crandall and Kenneth Flamm (Washington, D.C.: Brookings Institution Press, 1989); and Victoria Shannon, "Bull S.A., the Computer Company, Aims to Emerge from Dependence on France," *New York Times*, August 25, 2003.

19. For more about the Taiwanese incentive programs, see Kenneth L. Kraemer, Jason Dedrick, Chin-Yeong Hwang, Tze-Chen Tu, and Chee-Sing Yap, "Entrepreneurship, Flexibility, and Policy Coordination: Taiwan's Computer Industry," *Information Society* 12 (1996): 215–49; and Fu-Lai T. Yu, Ho-Don Yan, and Shen-Yu Chen, "Adaptive Entrepreneurship and Taiwan's Economic Dynamics," *Laissez-Faire (Universidad Francisco Marroquin)* 24–25 (2006): 57–74.

20. See, for instance, Peter Gwynne, "Brittany Positions Itself to Attract Telecom R&D," *Research and Development* 38:9 (1996): 34–35; Roland de Penanros and Claude Serfati, "Regional Conversion under Conditions of Defense Industry Centralization: The French Case," *International Regional Science Review* 23:1 (2000): 66–80; and Organisation for Economic Cooperation and Development, *OECD Territorial Reviews: France* (Paris: OECD, 2006).

21. See, for instance, OECD, *OECD Territorial Reviews: France*, 46.

22. Ibid., 120.

23. This account is primarily drawn from Carol Leoning, "Housing Grants Misused Audit Says," *Washington Post*, May 9, 2000; Resources, Community and Economic Development Division, General Accounting Office, *Inventory of Self-Sufficiency and Economic Opportunity Programs* (Washington, D.C.: GAO, July 28, 1997); and Saundra Elion, "Tenant Opportunity Program Grantees, District of Columbia Housing Authority," *Audit Report Office of Inspector General* (U.S. Department of Housing and Urban Development, March 20, 2000).

24. Leoning, "Housing Grants Misused."

25. This account is drawn from James A. White, "Picking Losers: Back-Yard Investing Yields Big Losses, Roils Kansas Pension System—but Idea of Using Such Funds to Help Local Industries Still Intrigues Politicians—Now a Steel Mill Is Sitting Idle," *Wall Street Journal*, August 21, 1991; John Hanna, "KPERS Attorneys Place Damages from Investments at $524 Million," Associated Press, September 17, 1997; and John Hanna, "Litigation over KPERS Losses Ends after 13 years," Associated Press, September 12, 2003.

26. Figures 4.1 and 4.2 are compiled from the databases of VenturexPert.

27. An excellent review of these programs, including the Danish experience, is in two publications by the Organisation for Economic Cooperation and Development, *Promoting Entrepreneurship and Innovative SMEs in a Global Economy: Towards a More Responsible and Inclusive Globalisation* (Paris: OECD, 2004), and *Government Venture Capital for Technology-Based Firms* (Paris: OECD, 1997).

28. Claire Lelarge, David Sraer, and David Thesmar, "Entrepre-

neurship and Credit Constraints: Evidence from a French Loan Guarantee Program," in *International Differences in Entrepreneurship*, ed. Josh Lerner and Antoinette Schoar (Chicago: University of Chicago Press, forthcoming).

29. The articulation of this model in the economics literature is frequently attributed to Mancur Olson, *The Logic of Collective Action* (Cambridge: Harvard University Press, 1965); and George Stigler, "The Economic Theory of Regulation," *Bell Journal of Economics* 2 (1971): 3–21; its formal modeling to Sam Peltzman, "Towards a More General Theory of Regulation," *Journal of Law and Economics* 19 (1976): 211–40; and Gary S. Becker, "A Theory of Competition among Pressure Groups for Political Influence," *Quarterly Journal of Economics* 98 (1983): 371–400.

30. Megan Woolhouse, "$1 Billion Life-Sciences Bill Passes Senate," *Boston Globe*, June 13, 2008.

31. See the data in BHI Policy Study, *Police Details in Massachusetts: Protection or Perk?* (Boston: Beacon Hill Institute for Public Policy Research, Suffolk University, 2004).

32. See William J. Baumol, "Entrepreneurship: Productive, Unproductive, and Destructive," *Journal of Political Economy* 98 (1990): 893–921; and Kevin M. Murphy, Andrei Shleifer, and Robert W. Vishny, "The Allocation of Talent: Implications for Growth," *Quarterly Journal of Economics* 106 (1991): 503–30.

33. These evaluations are Xulia González, Jordi Jaumandreu, and Consuelo Pazó, "Barriers to Innovation and Subsidy Effectiveness," *RAND Journal of Economics* 36 (2005): 930–50; and Saul Lach, "Do R&D Subsidies Stimulate or Displace Private R&D? Evidence from Israel," *Journal of Industrial Economics* 50 (2002): 369–90.

34. This account is drawn from "$158 Million for Building on IT Strengths (BITS)," press release, Ministry for Communications, Information Technology and the Arts, Government of Australia, June 20, 1999; Econtech Pty Ltd, *Evaluation and Future of the BITS Incubator Program* (Canberra: Econtech 2003); Organisation for Economic Cooperation and Development, "Australia," http://www.oecd.org/data oecd/9/7/1952416.pdf (accessed August 9, 2008); Austrade, "Government Funding Programs for Australian ICT Companies," http://www.

austradeict.gov.au/default.aspx?ArticleID=2930#BITS (accessed August 9, 2008); and James Riley and Simon Hayes, "Incubators Toss 'Good Money after Bad'— Most of the Funding Spent on Management Fees and Advice," *Australian*, June 8, 2004.

35. Richard Alston, Minster for Communications, Information Technology and the Arts, "Alston Launches $78 Million Program to Assist IT&T Industries," media release, November 29, 1999, http://www.richardalston.dcita.gov.au/Article/0,,0_4-2_4008-4_14651,00.html (accessed January 27, 2009).

36. "Incubators Doing Their Bit," press release, Ministry for Communications, Information Technology and the Arts, June 2, 2004.

CHAPTER 5: THE NEGLECTED ART OF SETTING THE TABLE

1. This discussion is drawn from, among other sources, Garry Bruton, David Ahlstrom, and Kulwant Singh, "The Impact of the Institutional Environment on the Venture Capital Industry in Singapore," *Venture Capital* 4:3 (2002): 197–218; David Lammers, "Singapore Seeks High Profile Role in Chip Design," *Electronic Engineering Times* 1342 (October 11, 2004): 34; and Sandy Oh, "Giving Singapore a Silicon Valley Mindset," *Business Week Online*, http://www.businessweek.com/smallbiz/0008/an000811.htm (accessed October 23, 2008).

2. This tabulation is drawn from a large number of government web sites, as well as Francis C. C. Koh and Winston T. H. Koh, "Venture Capital and Economic Growth in Singapore," Singapore Management University working paper (2002) no. 21-2002; and conversations with Yinglan Tan.

3. Readers familiar with Singapore's structured society might wonder about the effectiveness of such efforts to introduce creativity.

4. This account has drawn upon Wayne Arnold, "Science Haven in Singapore; Luring Top Stem Cell Researchers with Financing and Freedom," *New York Times*, August 17, 2006; Paul Smaglik, "Singapore: Filling Biopolis," *Nature* 425 (2003): 746–47; and Michael Frith, "Sprawling Biopolis Jazzes Up Singapore's Science Scene," *Nature Medicine* 9 (2003): 1440.

5. See, for instance, Yukata Imai and Masaaki Kawagoe, "Business Start-Ups in Japan: Problems and Policies," *Oxford Review of Economic Policy* 16:2 (2000): 114–23.

6. Ronald J. Gilson, "Engineering a Venture Capital Market: Lessons from the American Experience," *Stanford Law Review* 55 (2003): 1067–1103.

7. Gilson's account is drawn from Ralf Becker and Thomas Hellmann, "The Genesis of Venture Capital—Lessons from the German Experience," in *Venture Capital, Entrepreneurship, and Public Policy*, ed. Vesa Kanniainen and Christian Keuschnigg (Cambridge: MIT Press, 2004), 33–67.

8. This discussion is drawn from Josh Lerner and Antoinette Schoar, "Does Legal Enforcement Affect Financial Transactions? The Contractual Channel in Private Equity," *Quarterly Journal of Economics* 120 (2005): 223–46.

9. "Innovation's Golden Goose," *Economist* 365:8303 (December 12, 2002): 3.

10. See, for instance, David C. Mowery, Richard R. Nelson, Bhaven N. Sampat, and Arvids A. Ziedonis, *Ivory Tower and Industrial Innovation: University-Industry Technology Transfer before and after the Bayh-Dole Act* (Stanford: Stanford University Press, 2004).

11. See Josh Lerner, "Venture Capital and the Commercialization of Academic Technology: Symbiosis and Paradox," in *Industrializing Knowledge: University-Industry Linkages in Japan and the United States*, ed. Lewis M. Branscomb (Cambridge: MIT Press, 1999), 385–409.

12. This account is based on Seragen's filings with the U.S. Securities and Exchange Commission. In a 1992 agreement with the State of Massachusetts' Attorney General's Office, the university agreed to make no further equity investments. The school, however, made a $12 million loan guarantee in 1995 (subsequently converted into equity) and a $5 million payment as part of an asset purchase in 1997.

13. Josh Lerner, "ARCH Venture Partners: November 1993," *Harvard Business School Case* (1995): no. 9-295-105.

14. See Gompers, Lerner, and Scharfstein, "Entrepreneurial Spawning."

15. James M. Poterba, "Venture Capital and Capital Gains Taxa-

tion," in *Tax Policy and the Economy*, ed. Lawrence H. Summers, 3 (1989): 47–67.

16. Paul A. Gompers and Josh Lerner, "What Drives Venture Capital Fund-Raising?" *Brookings Papers on Economic Activity: Microeconomics* (1998): 149–92.

17. See, for instance, John Armour and Douglas Cumming, "The Legal Road to Replicating Silicon Valley," working paper, Economic and Social Research Council, Centre for Business Research, 2001.

18. Organisation for Economic Cooperation and Development," *Venture Capital Policy Review: United Kingdom*, STI Working Paper 2003/1 (Paris: OECD, 2003).

19. See the international evidence, for instance, in Leslie A. Jeng and Philippe C. Wells, "The Determinants of Venture Capital Funding: Evidence across Countries." *Journal of Corporate Finance* 6 (2000): 241–89, which highlights the extent to which labor market rigidities can deter venture capital investment.

20. These estimates are from Thomas Åstebro and Irwin Bernhardt, "The Social Rate of Return to Canada's Inventor's Assistance Program," *Engineering Economist* 44 (1999): 348–61.

21. Ibid.; and Thomas Åstebro, "Profitable Advice: The Value of Information Provided by Canada's Inventor's Assistance Program," *Economics of Innovation and New Technology* 10 (2001): 45–72.

22. Dean S. Karlan and Martin Valdivia, "Teaching Entrepreneurship: Impact of Business Training on Microfinance Clients and Institutions," discussion paper, Economic Growth Center, Yale University (2006): no. 941. For an overview of other works, see J. Bennet and M. M. Banerjee, "Light at the End of the Tunnel: Using Qualitative Research to Evaluate Micro-Entrepreneurial Training Programs," working paper, Center for Women and Enterprise, 1999.

23. New Zealand Venture Investment Fund, *Progress and Achievement Report: 2003/04* (Auckland: NZVIF, 2004).

24. Josh Lerner, David Moore, and Stuart Shepherd, *A Study of New Zealand's Venture Capital Market and Implications for Public Policy: A Report to the Ministry of Research Science and Technology* (Auckland: LECG, 2005).

25. This point was originally made by Bernard S. Black and Ronald

J. Gilson, "Venture Capital and the Structure of Capital Markets: Banks versus Stock Markets," *Journal of Financial Economics* 47 (1998): 243–77.

26. These facts are from the Bombay Stock Exchange web page, http://www.bseindia.com/ (accessed September 14, 2008).

27. These facts are drawn from Felda Hardymon and Ann Leamon, "Motilal Oswal Financial Services—an IPO in India," *Harvard Business School Case* (2007): no. 9-807-095; and Lily Fang and Roger Leeds, "Warburg Pincus and Bharti Tele-Ventures," in *The Globalization of Alternative Investments: Working Papers*, ed. Anuradha Gurung and Josh Lerner (Geneva: World Economic Forum, 2008), 151–63.

28. Jeng and Wells, "Determinants of Venture Capital Funding."

29. The information in this paragraph is drawn from Graham Bannock and Partners, *European Second-Tier Markets for NTBFs* (London: Graham Bannock and Partners, 1994).

30. This history of the EASDAQ market is drawn from Josh Lerner, "European Association of Securities Dealers: November 1994," *Harvard Business School Case* (1995): no. 9-295-116.

31. Reena Aggarwal and James J. Angel, "The Rise and Fall of the Amex Emerging Company Marketplace," *Journal of Financial Economics* 52:2 (1999): 257–89.

32. This fact is taken from Ramana Nanda and Tarun Khanna, "Diasporas and Domestic Entrepreneurs: Evidence from the Indian Software Industry," working paper, Harvard University, 2007.

33. AnnaLee Saxenian, *Local and Global Networks of Immigrant Professionals in Silicon Valley* (San Francisco: Public Policy Institute of California, 2002).

34. Nanda and Khanna, "Diasporas and Domestic Entrepreneurs."

35. "Plans for Asia's Silicon Valley," *Australian*, November 27, 2001.

CHAPTER 6: HOW GOVERNMENTS GO WRONG: BAD DESIGNS

1. B. Ramasamy, A. Chakrabarty, and M. Cheah, "Malaysia's Leap into the Future: An Evaluation of the Multimedia Super Corridor," *Technovation* 24 (November 2004): 871–83.

2. Roziana Hamsawi, "Adviser—Need to Create an Innovative Work Culture," *Business Times*, September 28, 1999.

3. This account draws on, among other sources, Cris Prystay, "Malaysia Is Banking on Bio Valley Plans," *Asian Wall Street Journal*, November 19, 2001; National Biotechnology and Bioinformatics Network, "Future Plan: Introduction," http://www.nbbnet.gov.my/plan.htm (accessed August 5, 2008); "Commercial Initiative for Malaysia's BioValley," Hong Kong Trade Development Council, unpublished document, June 2004; Datuk Leong Ah Hin, "BioValley as It Was Envisioned," *New Straits Times*, April 20, 2005; David Cyranoski, "Malaysia Puts Biovalley Under Wraps" *Nature* 424 (2003): 118; and "Malaysian Biotechnology: The Valley of Ghosts," *Nature* 436 (2005): 620–21.

4. Carol Murugiah, "All States to Establish 'Bio-Valley' Hubs by 2006," *New Straits Times*, September 28, 2003.

5. This account is drawn from, among other sources, Jonathan Kent, "Reviving Malaysia's Hi-Tech Dreams," BBC News, June 8, 2006; "Amica Sues Govt US$200M, President Appeals for PM's Intervention," *Bernama Daily Malaysian News*, January 19, 2006; and Oxford Business Group, "New Technology Blues: Malaysia," http://www.oxfordbusinessgroup.com/weekly01.asp?id=1785 (accessed August 8, 2008).

6. "Net Value: Reviving MTDC," *Edge Malaysia*, July 20, 2004.

7. Scott Wallsten, "The Role of Government in Regional Technology Development: The Effects of Public Venture Capital and Science Parks," Stanford Institute for Economic Policy Research Discussion Paper (2001): no. 00-39.

8. Michael I. Luger and Harvey A. Gildstein, *Technology in the Garden: Research Parks and Regional Economic Development* (Chapel Hill: University of North Carolina Press, 1991), 71.

9. This account is drawn from Markku Maula and Gordon Murray, *Finnish Industry Investment Ltd: An International Evaluation* (Helsinki: Ministry of Trade and Industry, Government of Finland, 2003); and Reijo Vihko, et al., *Evaluation of Sitra, 2002* (Helsinki: Sitra, 2002).

10. This paragraph is based on Peter K. Eisinger, "The State of

State Venture Capitalism," *Economic Development Quarterly* 5 (1991): 64–76; and Peter K. Eisinger, "State Venture Capitalism, State Politics, and the World of High-Risk Investment," *Economic Development Quarterly* 7 (1993): 131–39.

11. The discussion of the European Seed Capital Fund Program is drawn from Gordon Murray, "The European Union's Support for New Technology-Based Firms: An Assessment of the First Three Years of the European Seed Capital Fund Program," *European Planning Studies* 2 (1994): 435–61.

12. See Andrew Carragher and Darren Kelly, "A Comparison of the Canadian and American Private Equity Markets," *Journal of Private Equity* 1 (1998): 23–39; Organisation for Economic Cooperation and Development, *Venture Capital Policy Review: Canada*, STI Working Paper (Paris: OECD, 2003): no. 2003/4; and Daniel Sandler, *Venture Capital and Tax Incentives: A Comparative Study of Canada and the United States* (Toronto: Canadian Tax Foundation, 2004).

13. This account is based on, among other sources, Katrina Onstad, "Nothing Ventured, Tax Break Gained," *Canadian Business* 70:11 (1997): 47–52; Canadian Auto Workers, *Labour-Sponsored Funds: Examining the Evidence* (Toronto: CAW Research Department, 1999).

14. The statistics in this paragraph are from Douglas Cummings and Jeffrey MacIntosh. "Crowding Out Private Equity: Canadian Evidence," *Journal of Business Venturing* 21 (2006): 569–609.

15. Ibid.

16. "Government Sponsored Venture Capital in Canada: Effects on Value Creation, Competition and Innovation," working paper, University of British Columbia, 2008.

17. This figure is compiled from various publications and web sites of the Canadian, European, Israeli, and U.S. (National) venture capital associations, as well as those of the *Asian Venture Capital Journal*. In some nations where venture capital investments are not clearly delineated, I employ seed and start-up investments. The GDP data are from the Central Intelligence Agency, *2008 World Factbook*.

18. SDC Thomson, "VentureXpert," http://vx.thomsonib.com/NA-SApp/VxComponent/VXMain.jsp (accessed July 5, 2008).

19. Wim Borgdorff, "Public Money Is Harming the VC Industry," *Financial Times*, February 16, 2004.

20. Marco Da Rin, Giovanna Nicodano, and Alessandro Sembenelli, "Public Policy and Creation of Active Venture Capital Markets," *Journal of Public Economics* 90 (2006): 1699–1723.

21. See, for instance, the history of the Victorian Economic Development Corporation in Australia in Christopher C. Golis, *Enterprise and Venture Capital: A Business Builder's and Investor's Handbook* (London: Allen and Unwin, 2002).

22. Amar Bhidé, *The Origin and Evolution of New Businesses* (New York: Oxford University Press, 2000).

23. Paul A. Gompers and Josh Lerner, *Capital Formation and Investment in Venture Markets: A Report to the NBER and the Advanced Technology Program*, Report GCR-99-784 (Washington, D.C.: Advanced Technology Program, National Institutes of Standards and Technology, U.S. Department of Commerce, 1999).

24. This account is based on, among other sources, Donna Block, "The Venture Trap," *Deal Newsweekly* 4:40 (October 30, 2006): 39; House Committee on Small Business, Full Committee Hearing on "Legislation to Reauthorize the Small Business Innovation Research (SBIR) Program," March 13, 2008; and David T. Ralston Jr. and Stephen B. Maebius, "SBA Regulatory Change Enhances the SBIR Program and Provides New Investment Opportunities for Venture Capital Firms in SBIR Participants," in *Legal News: Nanotechnology* (Boston: Foley and Lardner, 2005).

25. American Small Business League, "Obama May Support Venture Capitalists' Move to Dominate Government Small Business Programs," http://www.asbl.com/showmedia.php?id=1272 (accessed May 1, 2009).

26. Statement of Mark G. Heesen, President, National Venture Capital Association, House Committee on Small Business, "Legislation to Reauthorize."

27. This figure is based on the data in Josh Lerner, "The Government as Venture Capitalist: The Long-Run Effects of the SBIR Program," *Journal of Business* 72 (1999): 285–318.

28. See Maryann P. Feldman and Johanna L. Francis, "Fortune Favors the Prepared Region: The Case of Entrepreneurship and the Capitol Region Biotechnology Cluster," *European Planning Studies* 11 (2003): 765–88.

29. See, for instance, the saga of Cleveland's biotechnology initiative as related in Michael Fogarty and Amit Sinha, "Why Older Industrial Regions Can't Generalize from Route 128 and Silicon Valley: University-Industry Relationships and Regional Innovation Systems," in Branscomb, *Industrializing Knowledge*, 473–509.

30. Lynne G. Zucker, Michael R. Darby, and Marilyn B. Brewer, "Intellectual Human Capital and the Birth of U.S. Biotechnology Enterprises," *American Economic Review* 88 (1998): 290–306.

31. For a discussion, see, for instance, Kenneth L. Kraemer, "Entrepreneurship, Flexibility, and Policy Coordination: Taiwan's Computer Industry," *Information Society* 12 (1996): 215–49; and Carol Yeh-Yun Lin, "Success Factors of Small- and Medium-Sized Enterprises in Taiwan," *Journal of Small Business Management* 36:4 (1998): 43–56.

32. For a detailed history and analysis of the program, see Lerner, Moore, and Shepherd, *New Zealand's Venture Capital Market*.

CHAPTER 7: HOW GOVERNMENTS GO WRONG: BAD IMPLEMENTATION

1. This account is drawn from Discovery Fund, "What Is Discovery Fund?" www.discovery-fund.com (accessed August 9, 2008); Judith Messina, "Misadventures of a Venture Fund: After Three Years, Big Apple Investment Can't Point to Much," *Investment News*, posted at http://www.investmentnews.com/apps/pbcs.dll/article?AID=/19980511/SUB/805110736/1009/TOC&ht= (accessed October 24, 2008); Michael Brick, "Business; Venture (Widely) Forth with City Hall Capital," *New York Times*, May 30, 1999; Matthew Flamm, "Gaining New Focus from Losses: Discovery Fund Ventures Near Home," *Crain's New York Business* 17 (April 23, 2001): 26.

2. Michael Selz, "Post Mortem: Leadership, Too Late—Pseudo Programs Spent a Lot of Its Venture Capital before Seasoned Management Arrived," *Wall Street Journal*, November 27, 2000.

3. Brick, "Business; Venture (Widely) Forth."

4. This account is based on "Iowa Suit Tests LPs' Authority to Abolish Fund," *Private Equity Analyst* 4 (1994): 1, 9.

5. See the discussion in David L. Barkley, Deborah M. Markey, and Julia Sass Rubin, "Certified Capital Companies (CAPCOs): Strengths and Shortcomings of the Latest Wave in State-Assisted Venture Capital Programs," *Economic Development Quarterly* 15 (2001): 350–66.

6. Lerner, Schoar, and Wongsunwai, "Smart Institutions, Foolish Choices." The results discussed here are from the National Bureau of Economic Research working paper, which used a larger sample than the published paper.

7. This discussion is drawn from Paul A. Gompers and Josh Lerner, *The Money of Invention* (Boston: Harvard Business School Press, 2001).

8. This account of Celltech's history is drawn from, among other sources, David Dickson, "Boom Time for British Technology?" *Science* 224:4645 (April 13, 1984): 136–38; Erik Ipsen, "Celltech Refuels Europe's Biotech Dream," *International Herald Tribune*, November 9, 1993; and Peter Mitchell, "Celltech Acquisition Sends Mixed Messages," *Nature Biotechnology* 22 (2004): 787.

9. Vanessa Maybeck and William Bains, "Small Company Mergers—Good for Whom?" *Nature Biotechnology* 24 (2006): 1343–48.

10. See the discussion, for instance, in Miguel Helft, "A Kink in Venture Capital's Gold Chain," *New York Times*, October 7, 2006.

11. "Testimony of William F. Dunbar," Subcommittee on Government Programs, Committee on Small Business, U.S. House of Representatives, "Venture Capital Marketing Association Charter Act," April 18, 1996. For other discussions of this proposal, see also White House Conference on Small Business, *The 60 Recommendations* (Washington, D.C.: Office of Advocacy of the U.S. Small Business Administration, 1996); and Division of Corporation Finance, U.S. Securities and Exchange Commission, "Final Report of the SEC Government-Business Forum on Small Business Capital Formation," June 1997.

12. For a review of the institutional challenges associated with state-sponsored Chinese venture funds and the failure to undertake evaluations, see Dai Zhi-min and Yu Jin-jin, "On the Institutional Defect

and Its Correction of Venture Capital in China," *Journal of Zhejiang University (SCIENCE)* 2:4 (2001): 462–66.

13. "Israeli Government to Sell Off Venture Capital Fund," Reuters, October 9, 1996.

14. See, for instance, Charles W. Wessner, ed., *The Small Business Innovation Research Program: An Assessment of the Department of Defense Fast Tract Initiative* (Washington, D.C.: Board on Science, Technology, and Economic Policy, Policy Division, National Research Council, 2000).

15. This problem was first identified by Linda R. Cohen and Roger G. Noll, eds., *The Technology Pork Barrel* (Washington, D.C.: Brookings Institution, 1991); and Scott J. Wallsten, "The Effects of Government-Industry R&D Programs on Private R&D: The Case of the Small Business Innovation Research Program," *RAND Journal of Economics* 31 (2000): 82–100.

16. Gompers and Lerner, *Capital Formation and Investment.*

17. Morten T. Hansen, Nitin Nohria, and Jeffrey A. Berger, *The State of the Incubator Marketspace*, Harvard Business Review Report (Boston: Harvard Business School Publishing, 2000): no. 4797.

18. See the discussion in Adam B. Jaffe, "Building Program Evaluation into the Design of Public Research Support Programs," *Oxford Review of Economic Policy* 18 (2002): 22–34, 33.

19. This account is drawn from, among other sources, Daniel Roth, "Catch Us If You Can," *Fortune* 149:3 (February 9, 2004): 65–74; and Adam Lashinsky, "Venture Capital Is Not for Girlie Men," *Fortune* 152:8 (October 17, 2005): 38.

20. These statistics are taken from various yearbooks of the European Venture Capital Association.

21. The discussion of Yozma is based on Gil Avnimelech, Martin Kenney, and Morris Teubal, "Building Venture Capital Industries: Understanding the U.S. and Israeli Experiences," BRIE Working Paper (2004): no. 160; Organisation for Economic Cooperation and Development, *Venture Capital Policy Review: Israel*, STI Working Paper (Paris: OECD, 2003): no. 2003/3; and Manuel Trajtenberg, "Government Support for Commercial R&D: Lessons from the Is-

raeli Experience," *Innovation Policy and the Economy* 2 (2002): 79–134.

22. Jerusalem Institute of Management, *Export-Led Growth Strategy for Israel* (Jerusalem: Jerusalem Institute of Management and the Telesis Group, 1987).

23. Yigdal Erlich, "The Yozma Group—Policy and Success Factors," http://www.insme.org/documenti/Yozma_presentation.pdf (accessed July 5, 2008).

24. This discussion of the Japanese case is based on Lerner, Branstetter, and Nakabayashi, "New Business Investment Company," and the sources cited therein.

25. See AusIndustry, "Fact Sheet: Venture Capital Limited Partnerships," http://www.ausindustry.gov.au/library/Fact_Sheet_VCLP_FINAL_Jan0820080115044831.pdf (accessed July 13, 2008); and Josh Lerner and Brian Watson, "The Public Venture Capital Challenge: The Australian Case," *Venture Capital* 10 (2008): 1–20.

26. Christian Keuschnigg, "Optimal Public Policy for Venture Capital Backed Innovation," working paper series, Department of Economics, University of St. Gallen (2005): no. 2003-09. For an interesting discussion of the policies implications of this and related papers (which I found very helpful in writing this section), see Andrew Gawith, Adolf Stroombergen, and David Grimmond, *New Zealand's Angel Capital Market: The Supply Side* (Wellington, New Zealand: Infometrics, 2004), appendix III.

CHAPTER 8. THE SPECIAL CHALLENGES OF SOVEREIGN FUNDS

1. These tables are based on, among other sources, Private Equity Intelligence, *Preqin Sovereign Wealth Fund Review* (London: Preqin, 2008); David G. Fernandez and Brenhard Eschweiler, *Sovereign Wealth Funds: A Bottom-Up Primer* (Singapore: JPMorgan Research, 2008); and the author's analyses.

2. Fernandez and Eschweiler, *Sovereign Wealth Funds*.

3. See, for instance, Stephen Jen, *How Big Could Sovereign Wealth*

Funds Be by 2015? (New York: Morgan Stanley Research—Global, 2007).

4. This account is based on, among other sources, Private Equity Intelligence, *Sovereign Wealth Fund Review*.

5. This account, among other sources, is drawn from Kyle Pope, "Uneasy Boom: Norway's Oil Bonanza Stirs Fears of a Future When Wells Run Dry—as Output Climbs, Many Say Money Is Being Wasted and a Slump Lies Ahead—a Town's Varying Fortunes," *Wall Street Journal*, October 3, 1995; and Svein Gjedrem, "The Management of Petroleum Wealth," lecture at the Polytechnic Association, November 8, 2005.

6. Quoted in David S. Landes, *The Wealth and Poverty Of Nations: Why Some Are So Rich and Some So Poor* (New York: Norton, 1998), 172.

7. *American Economic Review Papers and Proceedings* 82:2 (May 1997): 178–83.

8. For an overview of these issues, see Jeffrey D. Sachs and Andrew M. Warner, "The Curse of Natural Resources," *European Economic Review* 45 (May 2001): 827–38.

9. Lawrence Summers, "Funds That Shake Capitalist Logic," *Financial Times*, July 29, 2007.

10. William Miracky, Davis Dyer, Drosten Fisher, Tony Goldner, Loic Lagarde, and Vicente Piedrahita, *Assessing the Risks: The Behaviors of Sovereign Wealth Funds in the Global Economy* (Boston: Monitor Group, 2008).

11. "Bogus Backlash: Attacks by a Leading German Politician on Investors Have Been Hysterical and Misguided," *Economist* 375:8425 (May 7, 2005): 12–13.

12. These results are reported in Steven Davis, John Haltiwanger, Ron Jarmin, Josh Lerner, and Javier Miranda,, "Private Equity and Employment," unpublished working paper, University of Chicago, University of Maryland, U.S. Bureau of the Census, and Harvard University, 2008; and Josh Lerner, Morten Sorenson, and Per Stromberg, "Private Equity and Long-Run Investment: The Case of Innovation," working paper, Harvard University, Columbia University, and Swedish Institute for Financial Research, 2008.

13. These accounts are from, among other sources, Mark Landler, "Selling Oil Is Easier Than Investing Ethically, Norway Funds," *International Herald Tribune*, May 2, 2007; and "Asset-Backed Insecurity," *Economist* 386:8563 (January 19, 2008): 78–80.

14. Josh Lerner, Antoinette Schoar, and Jialan Wang, "The Secrets of the Academy: The Drivers of University Endowment Success," *Journal of Economic Perspectives* 22:3 (2008): 207–22.

15. Paul Gompers and Josh Lerner, "Money Chasing Deals? The Impact of Fund Inflows on Private Equity Valuation," *Journal of Financial Economics* 55:2 (2000): 281–25.

16. This account is drawn from "Manifold Effects of Hard Times," *Time*, December 9, 1974, 40–41; and Christopher Shea, "U. of Rochester to Cut Programs, Faculty, and Enrollment," *Chronicle of Higher Education* 42:16 (1995); A33; and personal conversations.

17. This account is based on Kevin Book, Felda Hardymon, Ann Leamon, and Josh Lerner, "In-Q-Tel," *Harvard Business School Case* (2005): no. 9-804-146; Business Executives for National Security, *Accelerating the Acquisition and Implementation of New Technologies for Intelligence: The Report of the Independent Panel on the Central Intelligence Agency In-Q-Tel Venture* (Washington, D.C.: BNES, 2001); and assorted press accounts.

18. Book et al., "In-Q-Tel," 11.

19. These quotes are drawn from one of several pieces on In-Q-Tel done by the paper: Christopher Byron, "Penny Stock Spies," *New York Post*, April 25, 2005.

20. This account draws on, among other sources, Annika Sundén, "The Swedish NDC Pension Reform," *Annals of Public and Cooperative Economics* 69 (1998): 571–83; and Karen M. Anderson, "Pension Politics in Three Small States: Denmark, Sweden and the Netherlands," *Canadian Journal of Sociology* 29:2 (2004): 289–312.

21. Government of Singapore Investment Corporation, "Structure," http://www.gic.com.sg/aboutus_structure.htm (accessed July 24, 2008).

INDEX

225